Recipes From and For the Garden

NUMBER FORTY-FOUR

W. L. Moody Jr. Natural History Series

Victor Z Martin
2010

Recipes From and For the Garden

HOW TO USE AND ENJOY YOUR BOUNTIFUL HARVEST

Judy Barrett

Art by Victor Z. Martin

TEXAS A&M UNIVERSITY PRESS   *College Station*

Copyright © 2012 by Judy Barrett
Manufactured in China by Everbest Printing Co.,
through FCI Print Group
All rights reserved
First edition

This paper meets the requirements of ANSI/NISO Z39.48-1992
(Permanence of Paper).
Binding materials have been chosen for durability.

♾

Library of Congress Cataloging-in-Publication Data

Barrett, Judy, 1945–
    Recipes from and for the garden : how to use and enjoy your bountiful
harvest / Judy Barrett ; art by Victor Z. Martin.—1st ed.
        p. cm.—(W.L. Moody Jr. natural history series ; no. 44)
    Includes index.
    ISBN 978-1-60344-578-8 (book/flexbound (with flaps) : alk. paper)—
    ISBN 978-1- 60344-659-4 (ebook format/ebook—p)
    1. Cooking (Natural foods)   2. Cooking (Vegetables)   3. Cooking
(Fruit)   4. Vegetable gardening.   5. Naturopathy.   6. Natural pesticides.
I. Title.   II. Series: W.L. Moody, Jr., natural history series ; no. 44.
    TX741.B3685   012
    641.3'02—dc23
    2011024033

Art by Victor Z. Martin

Contents

Victor Z Martin
2007

Preface

WHY A MIXED-UP GARDEN
IS THE VERY BEST KIND

A bountiful garden is a wonderful thing. It not only provides fresh food but a wealth of other things. A diverse garden has plants that are great for making into relaxing or invigorating teas for the gardener. Other plants can be made into teas that repel pests in the garden or feed the growing plants there. You can make insect repellants for when you are playing outdoors or salves for when you played too long. Lotions, potions, and remedies are all born in the garden. Certainly, there is no end to the good food a garden can provide—for both now and later. Jams, jellies, vinegars, and herbal blends are all great to enjoy throughout the year and share with friends as gifts. Whether you cook from your garden or eat the produce raw, a garden is a delightful source of health and nourishment for both the body and the soul.

Now, the kind of garden we're talking about here is not just landscape, although it is certainly that—and beautiful landscape as well. No, the kind of garden we're talking about is one with which the gardener is intimately involved. Whether it is a single flowerpot or 10 acres of crops doesn't really matter. What matters is that you choose the plants yourself, look after them (although a little help can't hurt) and decide how and when to use them.

A truly bountiful garden contains all sorts of plants: herbs, flowers, vegetables, trees, shrubs, fruit, berries, nuts, roses, perennials, and annuals. Whatever you like goes into your garden. There is no reason not to plant beans in the front yard or garlic under the peaches. The stodgy idea that gardens must be orderly creations just doesn't hold true. Herbs don't belong only in herb gardens. They belong in flower borders, vegetable beds, and pots on the porch. Roses like to mix it up with annuals and perennials and especially with onions and chives.

This book is a collection of garden recipes—for things that you harvest from the garden and things that you return to the garden to make it healthier and more productive and enjoyable.

Recipes From and For the Garden

Recipes for Things to Eat

Some Common and Uncommon Goodies from the Garden

Usually the bounty of the garden is best eaten right off the vine or with a slight steaming or quick sauté. Fresh vegetables are so full of flavor and crunch and enjoyment that they need little more than a quick washing to make them perfect. During the peak of gardening season, though, we get a little weary of grazing, so we start to look for some variety to feed ourselves and our family and friends. These recipes are designed to provide that variety. They are, for the most part, very simple recipes. I find that browsing through magazines and books and looking at recipes is fun, but it rarely leads to activity in the kitchen. So many recipes take time and effort that I'd rather spend elsewhere in the good old summertime. So I've looked for recipes I think you will actually use and enjoy. Many of them are easily adapted to your family's specific tastes. You can adjust the ingredients depending on what's ripe and what you like. There are a jillion recipes in the world—these are just a few that take advantage of the wonderful tastes available right in your own back yard. Almost all of them contain more than one vegetable or fruit; the organization is rather whimsical, so just browse until you find something that sounds good to you. Some of the recipes are old family favorites; others I've made up. Still more come from other cooks and gardeners and from historic recipe books online. Included are also some basic gardening tips to get your produce off to a good start.

Victor X. Martini
2009

Beans

Whether you grow beans to eat green, fresh shelled, or dried, the culture is the same. Plant in early spring and give plenty of rich soil and sunshine to make the plants healthy. Pole beans can grow on fences, trellises or other supports. Bush beans will hold themselves up. Pick green beans often to keep them producing and use at the peak of their flavor. Leave beans on longer to let the seeds mature in the pods if you plan to shell them. Let beans completely dry on the vine to store dried or to save as seeds. All beans are a great source of fiber, and shelled and dried beans produce nice vegetable protein in your diet. If you can't grow enough, visit the farmers' market regularly.

SWISS GREEN BEANS

1½ pounds fresh, whole green beans, cleaned and with strings
  removed

DRESSING:
5 tablespoons fresh lemon juice
2 large garlic cloves, freshly crushed
½ cup olive oil
1 tablespoon red wine vinegar
½ teaspoon dried or 2 teaspoons fresh tarragon or Mexican mint
  marigold
½ teaspoon dried or 1 tablespoon fresh dill weed
½ teaspoon salt
Freshly ground pepper
2 teaspoons prepared dark or Dijon mustard
½ cup packed minced fresh parsley

OPTIONAL:
⅓ pound Swiss cheese in thin strips
½ cup sliced ripe olives
½ cup each thinly sliced green and red peppers
½ cup chopped toasted almonds

Steam the beans until just tender. Remove from heat and immediately
rinse in cold water.

While the beans are cooking, combine the dressing ingredients in
a large bowl. Mix well to thoroughly combine. Add the rinsed, well-
drained beans to the dressing. Add Swiss cheese. Toss until dressing is
well distributed. Cover tightly and marinate 2–3 hours, stirring about
once an hour. Add olives and sliced peppers. Mix well; cover and chill
overnight or at least 5 hours. Serve topped with almonds.

GARLICKY GREEN BEANS

    2 cups fresh green beans, washed and trimmed
    2 tablespoons olive oil
    2 garlic cloves, minced
    2 tablespoons water
    Salt and pepper to taste

Put oil into a large skillet and sauté garlic over medium heat until the garlic begins to smell wonderful. Add the beans and toss to coat. Cook for a couple of minutes, then add water. Cover the pan and reduce heat to low. Cook gently until the beans are the desired tenderness. Season with salt and pepper and serve.

DILLY BEANS

    1 pound fresh green beans

    DILLED BUTTER:
    1 pound butter, softened
    3 bunches fresh dill
    1½ tablespoons minced garlic
    1 tablespoon lemon juice

Blend everything in a blender or food processor until well mixed. Shape the mixture into a roll and wrap it in parchment or waxed paper. Store in the freezer until ready to use.

Wash and trim the beans. Place the beans in a pot of boiling water and cook until they are crisp-tender. Drain beans in a colander. Place a chunk of dilled butter in a large skillet over medium heat and let it melt. Add the beans and heat through, stirring to make sure the beans are all coated with the butter. Serve when the beans are warm and well combined with the dilled butter.

BEAN AND
TOMATO SALSA

2 cups cooked fresh
   shelled or dried
   beans or rinsed
   canned beans (pinto,
   black, white, or
   whatever you have or
   like best)
2 cups fresh tomatoes,
   chopped (mixed
   colors are nice)
1 jalapeño pepper,
   seeded and minced
1 medium onion,
   chopped
2 garlic cloves, minced
Handful of chopped
   fresh cilantro
Juice of fresh lime
Salt and pepper to taste

Combine all ingredients
and serve as a salad on fresh greens or as dip with tortilla chips. If it
isn't spicy enough for you, add more or hotter peppers. Serve the salsa
at room temperature, but refrigerate any leftovers. (Omit the beans and
you'll have one version of plain old tomato salsa.)

MEXICAN BEAN MUSH

This is one of those recipes that can be a snack, an appetizer, lunch, dinner, or even breakfast. It is easy and tasty, and you probably have all the ingredients in the fridge and pantry.

2 cups mashed cooked beans (black, pinto, or whichever is your
  favorite)
2 tablespoons butter
½ cup tomato salsa (mild or hot, depending on your taste)
1 cup grated cheddar cheese (or whatever is in the refrigerator)
Tortilla chips

Melt the butter in a skillet and add the mashed beans. Mix and heat through, then add the salsa and cheese. Cook until the cheese is melted. Serve with crispy tortilla chips. If you are serving this dish at a party or on a buffet, sprinkle some grated cheese on top to make it look snazzier.

FRESH SHELLED BEAN SALAD

1 tablespoon olive oil
1 small onion, minced
3 garlic cloves, minced
1 bay leaf
4 cups fresh shelled beans or southern peas
2 cups chicken broth
4 medium tomatoes, sliced

DRESSING:
¼ cup olive oil
¼ cup red wine vinegar

Heat the olive oil over medium-high heat in a saucepan or skillet large enough to hold beans. Sauté the onion until tender. Add the garlic and bay leaf and sauté for another minute or so. Add the fresh shelled beans or peas and chicken broth. Bring to a boil and cover with the lid slightly ajar. Reduce the heat and simmer the beans until tender—about 25 minutes. Stir occasionally. Drain, remove the bay leaf, and pour the beans into a bowl. To make the dressing, whisk the oil and vinegar together; season with salt and pepper to taste. Pour the dressing over the beans while they are still warm.

Arrange the sliced tomatoes on a serving platter. Season with salt and pepper and ladle the warm beans over the tomatoes.

Store any leftovers in the refrigerator, but bring them to room temperature before serving.

GREENS AND BEANS

1 tablespoon olive oil
1 shallot, chopped
2 green onions, chopped
½ cup cooked or canned garbanzo beans, drained and rinsed
1 bunch spinach or chard, washed, torn, and large stems removed
1 tomato, sliced
Juice of ½ lemon
Salt and pepper to taste

Heat the olive oil in a large skillet. Stir in the shallot and green onions. (You can use a regular yellow or white onion if you don't have shallots or green onions.) Cook over medium heat until soft. Stir in the garbanzo beans and add salt and pepper. Place greens in pan and mix thoroughly with other ingredients. Cook until the greens are tender and wilted. Add tomato slices, squeeze lemon juice over everything and heat through. Add more salt and pepper, if needed.

Blackberries, Strawberries, and Blueberries

Berries are an essential flavor of spring and summer. Strawberries like pretty cool weather, so their season will be over early unless you freeze some. They prefer sandy soil. Blueberries want acidic soil and just won't produce without it. Long thought to grow only in northern climes, blueberries now come in varieties that flourish in Texas and other warm-weather states.

Strawberries will grow in most fertile soil, but in the South they have to be planted very early, and they rarely last more than a few years before new ones need to be planted. Some gardeners plant a new crop every year. You can also grow strawberries in containers—the traditional strawberry pot, of course, and hanging baskets and half-barrels are all good choices.

Blackberries will grow just about anywhere and are easily grown from bare root plants. When they are dormant, put them in the ground in an area with full sun. In areas where the ground does not freeze, they should be planted in late winter. Early spring is best for very cold areas. Blackberries will tolerate most kinds of soil, but they prefer a sandy mix. In heavy alkaline soils, the fruit will be less tasty and abundant, but it will still produce. If you add generous amounts of compost to your clay soil, the berries will do very well indeed. No matter the soil, good compost will encourage healthy growth.

The plants bloom with little white blossoms early in the spring, after which the fruit begins to grow. It is bright red at first and then ripens to a dark, almost black color. They are very sour before they are completely ripe, so be sure to wait! Berries won't ripen after they are picked.

All berries are packed with good nutrition—lots of vitamins, minerals, and antioxidants. A research study at Ohio State University found that blackberries are the most potent cancer-fighting berries of them all—by nearly 40%. Handle blackberries carefully; they are fragile. Just remove the hulls, wash them gently and let dry on paper towels. Put the berries into the freezer in plastic bags from which as much air has been removed as possible. The frozen berries will last a nice long time.

BERRY DELICIOUS BREAKFAST DRINK

½ cup strawberries
½ cup plain yogurt
½ cup blueberries
½ cup blackberries
½ cup milk

All ingredients should be chilled before blending. (You can use frozen berries for this.) Blend everything together on high speed until the berries are well smashed—about 30 seconds. Pour into 2 glasses and enjoy for breakfast or anytime you need a burst of flavor and energy.

BLACKBERRY LIMEADE

3 cups blackberries (save 8–12 berries for garnish)
6 cups water
⅔ cup lime juice
1 cup sugar
Ice

Blend the blackberries with 1 cup of water in a blender until totally puréed. Strain and press the juice through a fine-mesh strainer to remove the seeds.

Add the remaining water to the juice, then add the lime juice and sugar. Stir until the sugar is dissolved. Fill a glass with ice, pour in the juice and top with a slice of lime and a few berries for decoration.

A perfect summer treat. If you are lucky enough to have blackberries in the freezer, you can enjoy it the year around! You can also use lemons to make blackberry lemonade.

EASIEST BLACKBERRY COBBLER

2½ cups fresh or frozen blackberries
1 cup sugar
2 tablespoons flour
½ teaspoon cinnamon
1 tablespoon butter
1 double pie crust—either homemade or frozen

Spray a deep casserole dish with nonstick vegetable oil spray. Press one pie crust into the bowl so that it comes up the sides as far as it can. Mix together the berries, sugar, cinnamon, and flour and pour into the dish. Top with the other crust and crimp around the top edges to seal the two crusts with the dish. Open the top crust with decorative vents (or just poke a few holes) to let the steam escape and dot the top with the butter. Sprinkle the top with sugar and bake the cobbler in a 350°F oven until the crust is brown and the juice is bubbly, about 1 hour. Let it cool a while before serving. Serve with ice cream, whipped cream, sweetened heavy cream, or just by itself and it will be delicious!

If you have peaches that are ripe at the same time as the blackberries (or they cohabit the freezer together), they are great combined in cobbler.

BLACKBERRY SPINACH SALAD

    3 cups fresh spinach, washed and dried and torn into bite-size
        pieces
    2 cups fresh blackberries
    6 ounces crumbled feta cheese
    ¼ cup toasted chopped pecans or almonds
    1 small red onion, sliced into rings

Toss all the ingredients except the berries. Then add the berries so they won't get smashed. Offer dressing separately.

    DRESSING:
    ¾ cup extra-virgin olive oil
    ¼ cup lemon juice (or blackberry vinegar if you have it—
        see recipe on page 67)
    Salt and pepper to taste
    1 teaspoon sugar
    ½ teaspoon dried mustard

Mix together with a whisk or put into a jar and shake vigorously.

HONEY STRAWBERRY SALSA

    1½ cups diced sweet red pepper
    1 cup sliced fresh strawberries
    1 cup diced green bell pepper
    1 cup diced fresh tomato
    ¼ cup chopped Anaheim pepper
    2 tablespoons finely chopped cilantro
    ⅓ cup honey
    ¼ cup fresh lemon juice
    1 tablespoon tequila (optional)
    ½ teaspoon crushed dried red chili pepper

½ teaspoon salt
¼ teaspoon pepper

Combine all ingredients in a glass container; mix well. Cover tightly and refrigerate overnight to allow flavors to blend.

Serve with chips, or over grilled chicken or fish.

(From the National Honey Board, which offers lots of honey recipes at www.honey.com.)

STRAWBERRY OR BLUEBERRY PUDDING

Toast slices of bread and place in the dish from which they are to be served; over each slice pour enough canned strawberries or blueberries, thoroughly heated, to soften the bread. Serve hot. This is a delicious pudding, both easily and quickly made. When fresh fruit is used it should be stewed with enough sugar to sweeten it.

(From *The Woman Suffrage Cook Book,* 1886)

EASY BLUEBERRY CRUNCH

    4 cups fresh blueberries
    1 cup firmly packed brown sugar
    ¾ cup flour
    ¾ cup uncooked oats
    ½ cup margarine or butter, melted

Place the blueberries in a 2-quart baking dish; spread them evenly. Combine remaining ingredients and sprinkle over the berries. Bake for 45 minutes in a preheated 350°F oven. Serve warm or cool, with cream or ice cream, or plain.

BLUEBERRY PIE

2½ cups blueberries
½ cup sugar
⅛ teaspoon salt
Flour
Pastry for double crust

Line a deep plate with a single plain pastry crust, fill with blueberries slightly dredged with flour; sprinkle with sugar and salt, cover with another single pastry crust and bake 45 to 50 minutes in a moderate oven. For sweetening, some prefer to use one-third molasses, the remaining two-thirds to be sugar. Six green grapes (from which seeds have been removed) cut in small pieces much improve the flavor, particularly where huckleberries are used in place of blueberries.

(From *Boston Cooking-School Cook Book,* 1896)

Cucumbers

Cucumbers spell springtime and summer. They are cool, refreshing, and tasty, and at the same time they are easy to grow and enjoy. Like other vegetables, cucumbers like rich soil with plenty of compost and other organic material. They also need plenty of water since they are primarily made up of water themselves. You can grow cucumbers on a fence or trellis or in bush varieties in the garden or a big container. Give them plenty of sun and some love, and they will reward you with crunchy good low-calorie taste. Be sure to plant them as soon as the soil is warm because once it gets really hot, the cukes will become bitter.

If your cucumbers are young, they won't need peeling and seeding. If the seeds are large and the peel is tough, remove them during preparation.

CUCUMBER SALSA

  1 cup sour cream
  1 cup yogurt (low-fat is fine)
  ¼ cup chopped parsley
  ¼ cup chopped fresh cilantro
  1 teaspoon ground cumin
  ½ teaspoon salt
  2 cucumbers, peeled, seeded, and coarsely grated

Mix all ingredients. Cover and refrigerate until chilled, about 2 hours.
Serve by itself with chips or with grilled fish or chicken or grilled veggies.

FRESH SPRING CORN SALAD

  3 cups corn, cooked quickly and cut from the cob
  ¾ cups chopped cucumber
  ¼ cup chopped onion
  2 small tomatoes, chopped
  ¼ cup sour cream
  2 tablespoons mayonnaise
  1 tablespoon vinegar (any kind)
  ½ teaspoon salt
  ¼ teaspoon dry mustard
  ¼ teaspoon celery seed

Mix all ingredients and chill thoroughly. This salad tastes best if left to
mingle flavors overnight.

A VARIATION ON TABOULI SALAD

2 cups bulgur wheat (can be bought in bulk or in box)
2 cups very hot water
1 cucumber, chopped
2 tomatoes, chopped
4 green onions, sliced (some tops included)
½ cup sliced stuffed green olives
½ cup sliced black olives
½ cup chopped fresh cilantro
1 garlic clove, minced
¾ cups crumbled feta cheese
½ cup fresh lemon juice
½ cup extra-virgin olive oil
1 teaspoon pepper
2 teaspoons salt

Pour the hot water over the bulgur wheat in a large bowl. Let it sit until
the water is absorbed, about 30 minutes. If any water remains, drain it
away. Add the remaining ingredients and taste. Sometimes more lemon
juice or olive oil is needed. I don't know why it isn't the same every time,
probably something to do with humidity! Anyway, adjust moisture and
flavor to your taste and serve chilled or at room temperature. This is
a great side dish or main course. To make it heartier, you can also add
cooked beans, lentils, or chickpeas.

CUCUMBER SALAD DINNER IN A DISH

2 cooked chicken breasts, chopped
3 tablespoons olive oil
2 tablespoons lemon juice
Salt and pepper to taste
3 cups diced cucumbers
1½ cups cooked shelled beans or field peas (your favorite)
1 red bell pepper, chopped
½ cup crumbled feta cheese
2 tablespoons sliced black olives
2 tablespoons sliced stuffed green olives
¼ cup thinly sliced onion

Whisk the oil, lemon juice, salt, and pepper in a large bowl until combined. Add the remaining ingredients and toss to combine. Serve immediately or refrigerate if you prefer it chilled.

FRESH CUCUMBER SALAD

1 cup diced cucumber
⅓ cup diced red bell pepper
⅓ cup diced yellow bell pepper
¼ cup diced red onion
Juice of 2 limes
¼ cup chopped parsley
1 tablespoon rice vinegar
1½ teaspoons olive oil
Salt and pepper to taste

Combine all ingredients in a bowl and refrigerate at least 4 hours before serving. You can use whatever peppers you have—red, green, purple, or yellow—and you can add some hot peppers if that is to your taste. You can also add 2 cups cooked and cooled macaroni to make a heartier, whole-meal salad.

CUCUMBER-AVOCADO SOUP

1 large cucumber, chopped
1 ripe avocado, peeled and chopped
2 green onions, chopped
1 cup chicken broth
1 cup sour cream
2 tablespoons lemon juice
Salt and pepper to taste

Combine all ingredients in the jar or bowl of a blender or food processor. Blend until still slightly chunky. Chill thoroughly and serve on a hot summer day.

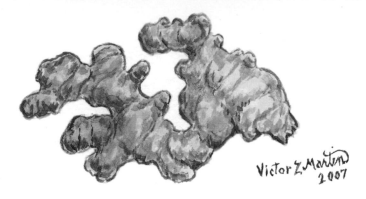

Victor Z. Martin
2007

Ginger

The ginger family is filled with beautiful and fragrant flowers that grace southern gardens during the hottest and most miserable season of the year. Exotic blooms and various-sized plants create a haven in the garden that makes summer tolerable.

But it is the least showy and most humble of the ginger species that makes your taste buds pop year-round. The culinary herb, *Zingiber offinale,* is a nice leafy plant in the garden, but the flower is less impressive than many of its ornamental cousins. Still, it is the root that we are interested in for kitchen use. You can plant ginger "hands" that you buy at the grocery store in the ground or in a container and soon have all the homegrown ginger you need.

Plant in rich soil and provide extra water when the weather is dry. Barely cover the rhizomes with soil and give the plants some protection from the afternoon sun. Harvest the root, once the plant is growing vigorously, by digging into the ground or container and breaking off a piece. Ginger must be protected from freezing, so mulch heavily or bring the container indoors in the winter.

Not just good, ginger is good for you, too. McCormick and the SuperFoods people have designated ginger as a "super spice" because it contains anti-inflammatory properties as well as antioxidants and other good things. While this is partly a marketing scheme, it is also based on tradition and modern research. Adding ginger and cinnamon to your diet seems to provide healthy benefits. After all, gingerbread was invented to settle the stomachs of overeaters centuries ago. For extra ginger taste, combine fresh, powdered, and crystalline ginger in recipes.

To substitute fresh ginger in recipes that call for dried, use 1 tablespoon grated fresh gingerroot for ⅛ teaspoon dried ground ginger.

CR   A note about molasses: Many times ginger and molasses are paired in recipes. They complement each other and create a wonderful flavor. The best kind of molasses to use in baking is made from cereal grain sorghum stalks that have ripened in the sun. This product is called molasses, sorghum, sorghum molasses, cane syrup, or sorghum syrup. Are you confused yet? It does not contain sulfur. The other common molasses is a by-product of the sugar-making process. It is bitter, usually treated with sulfur to keep it fresh, and usually darker in color than cane sorghum molasses.

Molasses in the garden is another matter. It comes in dry or liquid form and is an agricultural-grade product. (It is used as fertilizer and in animal food.) It is also made of sorghum cane or sugar cane. Either works for this purpose, but look for a product that does not contain sulfur.

MAKE YOUR OWN CANDIED (CRYSTALLIZED) GINGER

1 pound (500 grams) fresh gingerroot, peeled and thinly sliced

Place the sliced ginger in a heavy saucepan and cover with water. Cook gently until tender, about 30 minutes. Drain off the water.

Weigh the cooked ginger and measure an equal amount of sugar. Return the ginger to the saucepan and add the sugar and 3 tablespoons water. Bring to a boil, stirring often, and cook until the ginger is transparent and the liquid has almost evaporated. Reduce heat and cook, stirring constantly, until almost dry. Let the ginger cool.

Toss the cooled ginger in sugar to coat. Store crystallized (candied) ginger in an airtight container for up to 3 months.

(If you are inclined to travel sickness, take some of this candied ginger along in a sealed bag. It helps to chew on it when you get queasy.)

SALMON WITH GINGER

2 teaspoons olive oil
1 tablespoon honey
1 tablespoon Dijon mustard
2 teaspoons freshly grated gingerroot
1 pound salmon fillets

Preheat oven to 350°F. Mix together all ingredients except the salmon. Place the salmon fillets in a baking dish and brush the mixture evenly over them. Bake 14–20 minutes or until the salmon flakes easily with a fork. The thicker the fillet, the longer it will need to cook.

TRIPLE GINGER SNAPS WITH SORGHUM

These are the best-tasting ginger snaps I've ever had. Herbalist and author Susan Belsinger made them at a workshop at the Ozark Folk Center in Mountain View, Arkansas, and I just wanted to sit down and eat them all!

  2¼ cups unbleached flour
  1 teaspoon baking powder
  ½ teaspoon salt
  2 teaspoons ground ginger
  2 tablespoons finely chopped candied ginger
  1 cup unsalted butter, softened
  1 cup brown sugar
  ⅓ cup unsulfured sorghum molasses
  2 large eggs
  1 tablespoon freshly grated gingerroot
  1 teaspoon pure vanilla extract
  About ⅓ cup sugar

Preheat oven to 350°F. In a bowl combine the flour, baking powder, salt, ground ginger, and candied ginger. Toss well to mix.

In a food processor or mixer, cream the butter with the brown sugar until fluffy. Add the sorghum molasses and mix until combined. Add eggs, one at a time, until the dough is well mixed, then add the gingerroot and vanilla. Mix until combined. Add the dry ingredients and mix until just blended. If you have time, chilling the dough for a while will make it easier to handle and will also make the cookies rounded on top rather than flat.

Place the sugar in a saucer. Scoop the dough by the heaping teaspoonful and roll it into balls. Roll each ball in the sugar to coat and place them on a baking sheet at least 2 inches apart.

Bake in a preheated oven for 10 to 12 minutes or until cookies are light brown around the edges. Remove the pan from the oven and let the cookies stand for about 2 minutes. Remove the cookies onto a rack to cool. Store in a tightly closed tin for up to a week or freeze for up to 3 months.

JOE FROGGER COOKIES

The story is that back in colonial times, Black Joe's Tavern in Marblehead, Massachusetts, sold barrels of these oversized cookies to fishermen. The cookies would last for months at sea (getting harder and harder as time passed) and provide sustenance to the seamen.

This was a family favorite in my husband's Wisconsin family—the cookies probably were enjoyed by Great Lakes fishermen as well as Yankee revolutionaries.

½ cup shortening
1 cup sugar
1 cup dark, unsulfured sorghum molasses
½ cup orange juice (or water)
4 cups flour
1½ teaspoon salt
1 teaspoon baking soda
3 tablespoons freshly grated gingerroot or 1½ teaspoon ground
    ginger

½ teaspoon ground cloves
½ teaspoon ground nutmeg
½ teaspoon allspice
Granulated sugar for sprinkling

Cream the shortening and sugar until well blended. Stir in the molasses and orange juice. In another bowl, mix together the flour, salt, baking soda, ginger, cloves, nutmeg, and allspice. Blend a little at a time into the shortening mixture. Chill several hours or overnight so you can work with the sticky dough.

Preheat the oven to 375°F. Roll out the dough on a floured board or cloth until it is about ¼-inch thick. Cut with a big cookie cutter at least 3 inches in diameter—we always use a coffee can. Place on an ungreased cookie sheet and sprinkle with sugar. Bake for 10–12 minutes. They will not brown, but they become flat and sort of firm.

FRESH GINGER MINT TEA WITH HONEY

Making your own fresh tea is not only easy, it is healthier and much more economical. This one is delicious both hot and cold.

8–10 fresh or 2 tablespoons dried mint leaves
1 tablespoon honey—use local if possible
2 tablespoons peeled, very thinly sliced fresh gingerroot
2½ cups water

Place a medium-sized saucepan on high heat and add water. Bring water to a boil and add the ginger. Boil until the liquid is reduced by half. Strain the ginger, then add the ginger to the compost heap.

If using fresh mint leaves, chop and place in a tea strainer ball. Pour the honey in a large mug, then pour the steaming ginger water into the mug, stirring to melt the honey. Dunk the tea ball with mint leaves in it into the mug and steep for several minutes before drinking.

NATURAL GINGER ALE

1 teaspoon freshly sliced gingerroot or ½ teaspoon ground ginger
3 teaspoon red raspberry leaves
3 cups water
1 cup carbonated water
1 lemon slice

Combine the ginger, raspberry leaves, and water; bring to boil. Simmer 5 minutes. Remove from heat. Strain. Add the carbonated water and lemon slice just before serving over ice.

GINGER FRUIT PUNCH

1½-inch piece of fresh gingerroot
1½ cup water
3 cup green tea or hibiscus flower tea
6 ounces guava juice
¾ cup orange juice
¼ cup lemon juice
½ cup pineapple juice
Fresh peppermint

Peel and chop the gingerroot. Boil in ½ cup water until a strong flavor is obtained. Cool and strain the ginger through cheesecloth or coffee filter. Squeeze excess water from the ginger. Combine the ginger with the remaining ingredients except peppermint. Put a peppermint sprig in each glass with ice. Pour the fruit punch mixture over and enjoy.

Jujubes

If you think jujubes are sticky little candies you get in a box at the movie theater, you're only half right. Jujubes are also great landscape trees. They will grow in almost any area of the country, are easy and trouble-free in the garden, and produce tasty fruit.

Native to China, and also known as Chinese date trees, jujubes are small trees that are happy to grow in a wide range of conditions. They can take alkaline or acidic soils, rainy or dry conditions, high heat or extreme cold, and still produce their unusual fruit. The jujube tree grows 20–40 feet tall, but usually closer to 20 feet, and needs full sun. It thrives in areas where temperatures routinely rise above 100°F. and can stand subzero temperatures in the winter. They need only about 200–400 hours of winter chilling in order to fruit, so they are ideal for warm climates. They also bloom relatively late—in April or May—so they avoid problems caused by freezes that come in March and April.

In the first year or two after planting, the trees need some attention in the form of watering and protection from extreme temperatures while they are becoming established, but after that they are quite good at taking care of themselves. They need soil that drains well; they will not do well in areas where water stands around their roots. They are rarely troubled with disease or pest problems so are ideal for growing using organic methods. They require little fertilizer, although working compost into the soil makes for healthier, more productive trees.

Most people say that fresh jujubes taste like apples with a hint of date. Once they are dried, the date flavor becomes predominant. Two of the most popular varieties are Li and Shanxi Li, both of which are recommended for using both fresh and dried fruit. Li creates the largest fruit, generally about 2 inches in diameter. Check with local nurseries and growers to find out which variety grows best in your neighborhood.

Most jujubes will produce fruit on young trees. Some even fruit the first year they are planted, and most will fruit during the second year. Jujubes are self-pollinating, so you only need one tree to produce fruit.

The jujube fruit begins green and ripens from yellow to a rosy red shade. The fruit will dry naturally on the tree leaving little work besides harvesting for the gardener. It is not necessary to add sulfur or other drying material to the fruit for it to remain in good condition for dry use. If you live in a humid climate, you can harvest ripe fruit and complete the drying process in a low oven or dehydrator (some varieties dry better than others).

Jujubes are high in vitamin C and are packed with antioxidants. They have been used in Chinese medicine for thousands of years but are not widely known in the West. Like many other so-called super fruits, jujubes are catching on. Some studies say the jujube is helpful in attaining and maintaining overall good health and improving the immune system.

Just enjoying their flavor and the easy care of the tree are reasons enough to add jujubes to your landscape. The fruit is round or oval shaped and has a single seed in the middle which regrettably is not a freestone. It takes a little carving and coaxing to get the fruit away from the seed. You can also precook the fruit and remove the seeds from the cooked fruit. In either case, plan on taking a little time preparing the jujubes before you start the recipes. Measure the fruit for recipes after the seed has been removed. Jujubes can be eaten fresh or dried or added to recipes. Many people substitute the dried fruit in recipes containing raisins and eat them out of hand in the same way that they eat raisins. The fresh fruit can be substituted in recipes calling for apples and pears.

OATMEAL JUJUBE MUFFINS

   1 cup rolled oats
   1 cup plain yogurt or buttermilk
   ¾ cup flour
   ½ teaspoon baking powder
   ¼ teaspoon salt
   ¾ teaspoon baking soda
   ½ teaspoon cinnamon
   ⅓ cup packed light brown sugar
   2 eggs, lightly beaten
   ⅓ cup chopped dried jujubes

Preheat oven to 400°F. Combine the oats and yogurt and let stand 30 minutes. Meanwhile, sift together flour, baking powder, salt, baking soda, cinnamon, and brown sugar. Stir the eggs into the oat and yogurt mixture then add the sifted dry ingredients. Stir just until combined. The batter will be lumpy. Fold in the jujubes and spoon the batter into a muffin tin. Each muffin container should be about two-thirds full. Bake for 15–20 minutes.

MIXED JUJUBE SALAD

   4–6 cups fresh jujubes, cut in halves or quarters depending on size
      of fruit
   Juice of 1 lemon
   ½ cup sliced celery
   ½ cup chopped dried jujubes
   ⅓ to ½ cup mayonnaise

Sprinkle lemon juice on cut jujubes. Combine jujubes with celery and mayonnaise. Serve on lettuce leaves.

OVEN-BAKED JUJUBE MEATBALLS

1 pound ground beef, ground pork, ground lamb, or a combination
1 egg
2 tablespoons water
½ cup bread crumbs
¼ cup minced onion
¼ cup minced jujubes, fresh or dried
¼ cup grated Parmesan cheese
½ teaspoon salt
⅛ teaspoon pepper

Preheat oven to 350°F. In a large bowl combine the egg, water, bread crumbs, onion, jujubes, Parmesan cheese, salt and pepper. Combine well. Break ground meat into chunks and, working quickly, combine it with the other ingredients using your hands. (Overworking the meat makes it tough.) Form into meatballs about 1 inch in diameter and place on a wire rack in a broiler pan or any flat pan with sides to catch the fat that cooks out. Bake in preheated oven for 25–30 minutes until meatballs are cooked through. Cool and serve with your favorite sauce. You can double the recipe and freeze a batch for later use when time is of the essence.

TUNA SALAD

One 6 ⅛-ounce can chunk white tuna in water, drained
¼ cup diced apple
⅓ cup chopped jujubes, fresh or dried
2 tablespoons sliced celery
2 tablespoons sliced green onions
¼ cup mayonnaise (low-fat is fine)
2 tablespoons lemon juice
Salt and pepper, ¼ teaspoon each

Mix the tuna with the apple, jujubes, celery, and green onions. Stir in the mayonnaise, lemon juice, and salt and pepper. Serve on lettuce or spinach leaves for a salad or with lettuce or spinach in a pita pocket, or on whole-grain bread for a sandwich.

ZUCCHINI BREAD WITH JUJUBES

3 eggs
2 cups sugar
¾ cup vegetable oil
2 cups grated unpeeled zucchini
2 cups flour
1 teaspoon salt
1 tablespoon cinnamon
¼ teaspoon baking powder
2 teaspoons baking soda
1½ teaspoons vanilla
1 cup chopped nuts
¾ cup chopped dried jujubes (you can substitute raisins)

Beat the eggs well, then add the sugar and vegetable oil and continue to beat for a few seconds. Stir in the zucchini. Combine flour, salt, cinnamon, baking powder, baking soda, and add to the egg mixture. Add the vanilla, nuts, and jujubes (or raisins), stirring by hand to combine. Divide the batter into well-greased and -floured bread pans and bake at 350° for 55 to 60 minutes. Do not underbake. This is very moist bread. Makes two loaves.

APPLE JUJUBE MUFFINS

1 cup water
2 cups sugar
2 cups grated apples
2 cups chopped jujubes
1 cup butter
2 teaspoons ground cinnamon
2 teaspoons grated nutmeg
½ teaspoon ground cloves
1 cup pecans
2 teaspoons baking soda
3½ cups unbleached flour

Preheat the oven to 350°F.

Combine the water, sugar, apples, jujubes, butter, cinnamon, nutmeg, and cloves in a saucepan and bring to a boil. Remove the pan from the heat and let cool completely.

In a large bowl combine the pecans, baking soda, and flour. Add the cooled liquid mixture to the flour mixture and stir just until blended. Fill muffin tins and bake for 15–25 minutes depending on the size of your muffins.

Victor Z Martin 2010

Lemons

We have learned that it is possible to grow citrus in nontropical locations if we're agreeable to growing them in large containers and providing protection during the winter. In areas where the weather is warmer and where winters are less severe than they once were, some citrus can be grown outdoors in the ground. Meyer lemons are among the favorite citrus fruits grown by home gardeners. They have a wonderful juicy fruit that seems to combine the taste of lemon and orange and are beautiful plants with glossy leaves and sweet white blooms. Named after Frank Meyer, who brought the plant to the United States in 1908 from China, the Improved Meyer Lemon is now available in a dwarf variety that is perfect for container growing. Because these lovely lemons have a relatively thin skin, they do not ship well, so growing your own is the best way to have them!

Lemons and other citrus enjoy sun and warmth. They need rich soil and a reliable source of water. They flower and fruit at the same time, so they need lots of fertilizer. Use regularly an all-purpose fertilizer such as fish emulsion or rich compost or a nice organic blend of nutrients. In a container, they will need feeding monthly. To maximize absorption, feed about two hours after watering thoroughly.

Most lemons ripen in the late fall through the winter months. We usually have lemon pie for Thanksgiving and lemonade for any occasion. Don't forget to water even when the weather is cool.

LEMONADE

Who says lemonade has to be sweet? You can make a delightful summer-time drink with just lemon juice and water. If you really want it sweet, use a little stevia for sugar-free sweetness.

    4 ounces fresh lemon juice
    8½ cups of water

Mix and enjoy over ice. Use sparkling water for extra excitement. Studies suggest that, in addition to being refreshing and calorie-free, drinking lemon water regularly can help stave off the formation of kidney stones.

LEMON MERINGUE PIE

    2 large eggs, separated
    One 14-ounce can sweetened condensed milk (using fat-free
      works)
    ½ cup freshly squeezed lemon juice
    Grated rind of ½ lemon
    ¼ cup granulated sugar
    Baked regular pie crust or graham cracker crust

This pie is so easy it is ridiculous to include a recipe, but it is also so good I can't leave it out.

Preheat oven to 350°F. Combine the sweetened condensed milk and egg yolks. Stir in the lemon juice and grated rind. Pour into the baked crust.

Whip egg whites until they are almost stiff. Gradually add the sugar and continue to beat until egg whites are glossy and stiff. Pile on top of filling. Bake the pie in a preheated oven until the meringue is golden brown, about 10 minutes. Chill before serving.

LEMON ICE CREAM

Juice of 8 lemons
1 lemon, sliced very thin, and slices cut in half
3½ cups sugar
One 12-ounce can evaporated milk
2 cups buttermilk
1 teaspoon salt
½ gallon milk (whole, 2%, or 1%—any fat amount will work, but the higher the fat content, the richer the ice cream)

Combine the sugar and lemon juice and mix until the sugar is dissolved. Add the evaporated milk and buttermilk and mix well. Add the lemon slices and pour into the container of an ice cream maker. Insert the dasher, stir around with it, and then fill the container to the top with milk. Freeze according to manufacturer's instructions. If you can wait, pack the ice cream container in ice and salt for an hour or put it in the freezer for an hour to make the ice cream firmer. If you can't wait, slurp it down. The lemon pieces will freeze and be yummy!

STELLA'S SPICED TEA

6 quarts boiling water
1½ pounds sugar
2 lemons, washed and juiced, the rind reserved
4 oranges, washed and juiced, the rind reserved
4 whole cloves
8 sticks cinnamon
1 cup loose tea

Add the sugar, fruit juices, fruit rinds, cloves, and cinnamon to the boiling water. Let stand for 20 minutes. Keep hot but do not let it boil. Add tea. Steep for 5 minutes.
Strain and serve. Keep leftovers in the refrigerator and heat to serve.

LEMON CHICKEN

2 tablespoons lemon zest
⅓ cup lemon juice
2 garlic cloves, crushed or minced fine
2 tablespoons minced fresh thyme (lemon thyme is good)
2 tablespoons minced fresh rosemary
1 teaspoon salt
1 teaspoon black pepper

Combine all ingredients and place in a gallon freezer bag. Add 3–4 pounds of chicken pieces (not skinned or deboned). Pierce each chicken piece a few times with a fork or knife to allow openings for the marinade. Turn the bag around so that all the chicken pieces are coated with the marinade, then seal the bag. Place the bag of chicken pieces in a bowl in the refrigerator and let sit for at least two hours. If you open the refrigerator in the meantime, turn the bag a couple of times.

Preheat the oven to 425°F. Remove the chicken pieces from bag and place in a single layer in a large baking dish, skin side up. (Save the marinade.) Brush a little melted butter on each chicken piece. Bake for 25 minutes, then baste generously with the remaining marinade and return the chicken to the oven. The chicken should be done in about 50–55 minutes total, when the skin is crispy brown and the chicken is thoroughly cooked. Pour off the pan juices from the chicken, skim the fat from the top, and serve the sauce with the chicken.

CRISPY LEMON-PECAN FISH

1½ pounds fish fillets (catfish, tilapia, or your favorite)
1 cup milk
2 cups cornmeal
½ teaspoon salt
1 stick butter
1 cup olive oil
1 cup chopped pecans

1 cup chopped parsley
½ cup lemon juice

Wash the fillets and place them in a bowl with the milk. Let them soak for about 15 minutes, then remove from the milk and dip them in the cornmeal.

Heat 2 tablespoons of the butter and all the olive oil in a skillet over medium-high heat. Fry the fish until it is crispy and brown, about 2 minutes on each side.

Drain the fillets on paper towels and keep warm while cooking the remaining fillets.

Remove the oil from the skillet, reduce the heat to medium, and add the remaining butter. When the butter has melted, add the pecans. Stir constantly until they are nicely toasted and brown. Add parsley and lemon juice and stir until everything is mixed and warm. Pour the pecan and parsley mixture over the fish or serve it separately in a sauce bowl with the fish.

LEMON PASTA SAUCE

4 tablespoons butter
4 tablespoons flour
1 cup milk
2 garlic cloves, minced
1 cup chicken broth
4 tablespoons lemon juice
2 teaspoons lemon zest (or 1 teaspoon lemon and 1 teaspoon lime zest)
10 ounces uncooked pasta (your choice)

Start the water boiling for the pasta. Melt the butter in a large pan over medium heat and cook the garlic until tender and fragrant. Don't burn the garlic! Sprinkle the garlic with the flour and quickly combine. Slowly add the milk and chicken broth. Stirring constantly, cooking the sauce until it is thick and rich looking. Stir in lemon juice and zest. Meanwhile, the pasta should be done at the same time. (Try to keep the pasta from turning to mush before the sauce is done.) Add the pasta to the sauce and combine well.

You can serve the pasta with lemon sauce alone or stir in chunks of cooked meat or seafood for a main course. Really yummy. If it isn't lemony enough for you, add more lemon juice!

Spinach and Swiss Chard

Spinach is a cool-weather crop that you can keep going just about all winter if you grow it in a big pot and protect it on very cold nights. Grow spinach from seed in good, rich soil. Water it regularly when there's no rain, and feed it with liquid organic fertilizer about every two weeks. Snip off the older leaves as they mature so that the young leaves can grow.

Fresh spinach salad is always tasty and nutritious, but cooked spinach is good, too, especially in the winter when warm food keeps you feeling cozy. But remember to steam your greens quickly so as not to cook out all the nutrients (unless you plan to drink the pot likker). Spinach is a great source of all sorts of nutrients, including vitamins, protein, iron, and calcium. Use fresh spinach instead of lettuce on sandwiches to boost nutrition.

Swiss chard is really a member of the beet family, but it is a great substitute for spinach. It is packed with nutrients and is easier to grow in warmer climates. It will produce almost year-round. It resists pests and diseases and is a beautiful plant. People often mistake the red-stemmed varieties for rhubarb. Grow chard in the ground or in containers and give it plenty of compost and a steady source of water. Young leaves are great in salad, and the stalks can be chopped and cooked, or eaten like celery. In either case, if you want to be healthy, "Eat your greens!"

Greens pack more nutritional punch than most foods. They contain vitamin A, vitamin B6, calcium, magnesium, vitamin C, iron, manganese, potassium, folic acid, and PABA. Try getting all that out of a Pop Tart!

ORIENTAL GREEN SALAD

1 tablespoon vinegar (any kind)
1 tablespoon soy sauce
¾ teaspoon sugar
¼ teaspoon ground ginger
3 tablespoons olive oil
1 green onion, including top, minced fine
6 cups torn spinach or young chard leaves, or mixture of both
2 cups shredded Chinese cabbage
2 tablespoons toasted sesame seeds

In a salad bowl, blend the vinegar, soy sauce, sugar, and ginger. Stir in the oil and green onion. Add the spinach and cabbage and toss well. Sprinkle with the sesame seeds. Serve right away.

SPINACH ARTICHOKE CASSEROLE

Large bunch of spinach, chopped, cooked quickly, and drained
½ cup butter or margarine, melted
Two 8-ounce packages cream cheese
One 7¾-ounce can artichokes, drained and quartered
One 9-ounce can water chestnuts, sliced and drained
1½ teaspoons onion powder
Salt and pepper to taste
⅓ cup grated Parmesan cheese—reserve for sprinkling on top

Preheat oven to 350°. Mix all ingredients except cheese and place into 8 × 8-inch or 9 × 13-inch greased baking dish. If two small dishes are used, one can be frozen for later use. Sprinkle Parmesan on top and cover with lid or foil. Bake 40 minutes. Ingredients may be assembled the night before for baking the following day. Serves 10–12.

SPINACH AND STRAWBERRY SALAD

> 1 pound fresh spinach, washed thoroughly and large stems
>   removed, torn into bite-sized pieces
> 2 cups fresh strawberries, hulled and sliced
> 1 green onion, sliced thin with some green included

> DRESSING:
> ¼ cup vegetable oil
> ¼ cup lemon juice
> ¼ cup honey
> 1 tablespoon poppy seeds
> 2 tablespoons sesame seeds

Put the spinach, strawberries, and green onion into a large serving bowl.
Whisk together the dressing ingredients until thoroughly mixed. Pour
over the salad and toss so that all pieces are coated. Serve right away.

WILTED GREEN SALAD

> 8 cups mixed greens, washed, dried, trimmed, and torn into bite-
>   sized pieces

Place the greens in a salad bowl and refrigerate while making the dressing.

> DRESSING:
> 3 slices bacon
> 1 small onion, minced
> salt and pepper to taste
> 2 tablespoons red wine vinegar

In a medium skillet or saucepan, cook the bacon until crisp. Remove and
set aside. Add the onion to the drippings. Cook over medium heat until
the onion is translucent and tender. Add the salt, pepper, and vinegar.
Simmer briefly to mingle flavors, then pour over the mixed greens in the
salad bowl. Toss quickly. Crumble the bacon and sprinkle it on the salad.

VEGETABLE QUICHE

Quiche is an easy dish for an elegant-looking dinner or lunch in no time. Use a frozen crust to speed up the process and substitute your favorite veggies and cheese to add variety to the dish.

  1 uncooked piecrust
  1 pound fresh spinach, cooked and chopped
  ½ cup chopped green onion
  1 garlic clove, minced
  2 tablespoons butter
  1½ cup shredded Swiss cheese (6 ounces)
  3 eggs, lightly beaten
  ¾ cup milk
  1 teaspoon salt
  1 teaspoon dried or 1 tablespoon fresh basil
  ½ teaspoon celery salt
  2 medium tomatoes, sliced
  1 tablespoon grated Parmesan cheese
  1 tablespoon bread crumbs

Sauté the onions and garlic in the butter until they are golden. Add the cooked spinach. Stir constantly over medium heat until moisture evaporates. Combine with the cheese, eggs, milk, salt, basil, and celery salt. Turn into the pie shell. Arrange the tomatoes around the edge. Bake at 425°F for 15 minutes. Lower the heat to 350° and bake for 10 more minutes. Combine the bread crumbs and Parmesan cheese; sprinkle over the tomatoes. Bake 10 minutes more or until the top is puffy. Let it stand 10 minutes before serving.

SIMPLE WILTED SWISS CHARD

 2 tablespoons olive oil
 4 garlic cloves, minced
 1 bunch Swiss chard—chop the stalks and coarsely chop the leaves
 ¼ cup balsamic vinegar
 1 tablespoon lemon juice
 Salt and pepper to taste

Heat the oil in a large skillet over medium heat. Sauté the garlic and
the chopped Swiss chard stems until they become tender. Don't burn
the garlic! Add the chard leaves and vinegar and cook until the greens
are wilted and tender. Sprinkle on the lemon juice, salt and pepper, and
serve.

GREENS FOR BREAKFAST

Do you ever have a little dab of sautéed greens left over? Next time,
reheat the greens, pile them on a piece of toasted whole-grain bread, put
a fried egg on top, and cap with another piece of toast. You'll have a tasty,
highly nutritious breakfast sandwich that will stick with you all morning
long.

Summer and Winter Squash and Pumpkins

Squashes grow in virtually every part of the country where enough moisture is available. Squash is among the most versatile of vegetables. It can be eaten raw, steamed, fried, baked, pickled, or added to other ingredients to make great combinations. Summer squash is best eaten as soon as it is picked. Winter squash keeps well without refrigeration. Pumpkins are members of the squash family, and although lots of people use them for fall decorations, few cook and eat them—which is too bad! Pumpkins are full of nutrients, tasty and easy to cook.

Squash will thrive in any soil that is well drained and rich in organic material. Fairly heavy feeders, squash should be planted in soil that has been amended with compost or manure.

Plant squash seeds after the soil has warmed and all danger of frost is past. They come up quickly and are vulnerable to cold weather. Place six seeds in each hill and cover with an inch of soil. The hills should be spaced four to five feet apart. Once the seeds have sprouted and healthy young plants are growing, thin to two seedlings per hill.

Squashes need a steady supply of water as they grow. Drought will make the vines unproductive and the fruit tasteless and shriveled. A spraying of seaweed and fish emulsion will help the young plants set blooms and produce better. The flowers must be pollinated by insects, so if you start your seedlings under a row cover, remove the cover when flowers begin to appear.

The most common insect pests in squash are the squash vine borer and the squash beetle. The borer drills down the stem of the plant, causing the leaves to wither and die. If you see signs of a squash vine borer, slit the stem lengthwise at the injured point and remove the wormlike culprit. Cover the stem with soil so new roots can form. The squash beetle lays eggs on the underside of leaves. Eggs can be picked off by hand and crushed. If you use row covers when you first set out your plants, they will help deter insect pests, and as always, healthy plants are less attractive to bugs than are weak plants.

All squashes can be enjoyed while young and tender—including those generally known as winter squash. All types of squash produce well in the home garden, and as every gardener knows, zucchini produces best of all—sometimes producing more fruit than the gardener knows what to do with! Pumpkins can be cut in half, seeded, and baked in the oven in a pan with a little water in the bottom and foil over the top. The cooked pumpkin flesh is ready to eat mashed with butter, salt, and pepper (or cinnamon, sugar, and anything else you like) or you can use it in recipes. Growing and using your own is much more flavorful and economical than buying canned. You can substitute pumpkin for any kind of winter squash in recipes (and vice versa).

SQUASH MEDLEY

2 cups mixed summer squash, cut into ¼-inch slices
2 tablespoons olive oil
1 medium onion, chopped
1 sweet pepper, any color, chopped
1 large tomato, chopped
Salt and pepper to taste

Select young squash of as many kinds as you grow—yellow, zucchini, scallop, for example. Wash and cut the squash into ¼-inch thick slices. In a skillet, heat the oil over medium heat. Add the onion and sweet pepper and sauté until they begin to wilt. Add the squash and toss to make sure it is well mixed. Continue to cook until the squash is tender but still firm. Add the chopped tomato and cook until just warmed through. Add the salt and pepper and serve.

SOUTHWESTERN SQUASH CASSEROLE

2 small yellow squash, sliced
2 small zucchini, sliced
1 medium onion, sliced
2 garlic cloves, minced
2 tablespoons olive oil
1 mild to spicy chili pepper, seeded and chopped
2 cups yellow sweet corn
½ cup grated Cheddar cheese
½ cup grated Monterey jack cheese
1 teaspoon ground cumin

Put the oil in a skillet and lightly sauté the squash, onions, garlic, and chili pepper until just soft. Toss with the sweet corn, cheeses, and cumin; put in a large casserole dish that has been sprayed with nonstick vegetable oil spray. Bake at 400°F for 20–25 minutes until cheese is melted and everything looks hot and bubbly.

SQUASH AND TOMATOES WITH ALMONDS

2 tablespoons butter
¾ cup slivered almonds
3 teaspoons olive oil
2 pints cherry tomatoes
4 medium zucchini cut into ½-inch slices
1 teaspoon dried or 1 tablespoon fresh basil
1 tablespoon chopped parsley
1 teaspoon chopped oregano
¾ teaspoon salt
½ teaspoon pepper

In a skillet, melt the butter. Add the almonds and stir for 7 minutes over medium-low heat. Remove the almonds and drain on a paper towel. Add the olive oil to the skillet, then add the whole cherry tomatoes and zucchini. Stir over medium heat until the tomatoes are soft but not cracked (about 10 minutes). Sprinkle the tomatoes and zucchini with the basil, parsley, oregano, and the toasted almonds. Serve immediately.

SQUASH, CHICKEN, AND RICE CASSEROLE

    4 tablespoons vegetable oil
    2 cups chopped onion
    1 garlic clove, minced
    3 cups diced summer squash (yellow, zucchini, or other)
    2 cups sliced mushrooms
    3 cups diced cooked chicken
    1 cup uncooked rice
    2½ cups chicken broth or water
    1½ teaspoon fresh thyme or ½ teaspoon dried thyme
    ½ teaspoon dried or 1 teaspoon fresh ground rosemary
    ½ cup grated Parmesan cheese
    Salt and pepper to taste
    2 cups chopped tomatoes
    ¼ teaspoon chili powder

Preheat the oven to 350°F. Heat 3 tablespoons of the oil in a large skillet and sauté 1 cup of the onions with the garlic for 2 minutes. Add the squash and mushrooms and sauté for 3 minutes more. Add the chicken, rice, broth, thyme, rosemary, and cheese to the squash mixture. Season with salt and pepper. Place the mixture in a greased 9 × 13-inch baking dish.

For the topping, heat the remaining 1 tablespoon oil and sauté the remaining cup of onion for 3 minutes. Add the tomatoes and chili powder. Season with salt and pepper to taste. Spoon the topping over the chicken and rice mixture. Cover with a lid or aluminum foil. Bake for 1 hour or until rice is done.

STUFFED SQUASH

This is a good way to use those squashes that hide under the leaves until they get too big. This is a great entrée for lunch or dinner.

  2 large squashes
  2 tablespoons oil
  1 cup chopped onions
  ¼ cup pine nuts
  1 cup cooked rice
  1 cup tomatoes, chopped, peeled, and seeded
  ½ cup chopped parsley
  1 tablespoon chopped fresh mint
  Salt and pepper to taste
  Marinara, tomato, or spaghetti sauce

Cut the squash in half lengthwise. (It may not be easy.) Scoop out the seeds and cook the squash halves in boiling water until the meat is fork tender but the skin is still firm.

In a large skillet, heat the oil over medium heat. Add the onions and cook until tender. Add the pine nuts and cook for a few more minutes. Add the rice, tomatoes, parsley, and mint; heat through, stirring well.

Stuff the squash halves with the rice mixture. Place in a shallow baking pan and add about ¼ inch of water to the bottom of the pan. Cover with foil and bake in a preheated 400° oven for 30 minutes.

Serve with your favorite marinara sauce or homemade tomato sauce.

ACORN SQUASH RINGS

Trim the ends from two large acorn squash. Slice crosswise into ¼-inch-thick slices. Remove the seeds and fiber from the center. Place in one layer in a shallow baking dish that has been lightly buttered. Pour ⅔ cup orange juice over the squash. Sprinkle ¾ cup brown sugar and 1 teaspoon ground cinnamon. Dot with butter and sprinkle with salt. Cover with foil and bake at 350°F for 30 minutes.

BUTTERNUT SQUASH STUFFED WITH APPLES

2 butternut squashes, halved
    lengthwise, with seeds removed
3 tart apples, peeled and chopped
    Dash salt
¼ cup golden raisins (you could
    use jujubes)
¼ cup nuts—walnuts, pecans,
    almonds, or whatever you like
¼ cup brown sugar
¼ teaspoon cinnamon Butter

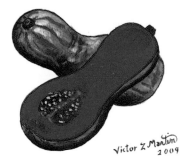

Mix the apples, raisins, nuts, brown
sugar, and cinnamon together. Stuff the
mixture into the center of the squash.
Pour about 1½ inch of hot water into a
baking pan and place the stuffed squash
into the pan. Cover tightly with foil and
bake at 350°F for 1 hour.

SPAGHETTI SQUASH WITH HERB SAUCE

1 3-pound spaghetti squash
1 tablespoon minced fresh parsley
2 teaspoon butter
½ teaspoon dried or 1 tablespoon fresh basil
⅛ teaspoon dried or 1 teaspoon fresh minced sage
¼ teaspoon salt
⅛ teaspoon pepper

Wash the squash. Cut in half lengthwise and remove the seeds and fiber.
Place the squash cut side down in a large skillet; add water to about 2
inches deep. Bring to a boil. Reduce the heat; cover and simmer until the
squash is tender, 20 to 30 minutes. Drain the squash and let it cool until

you can handle it. Using a fork, remove the spaghetti-like strands into a large bowl. Add the parsley, butter, basil, sage, and salt and pepper and toss gently. Serve with Parmesan cheese for sprinkling on top.

PUMPKIN PIE DIP

    8 ounces cream cheese
    2 cups powdered sugar
    2 cups cooked pumpkin, puréed
    1 teaspoon cinnamon
    ½ teaspoon ground ginger or nutmeg (or mixture of both)

Using an electric mixer, beat cream cheese and sugar at medium speed until smooth. Add pumpkin, cinnamon, and ginger or nutmeg (or use 1–2 teaspoons pumpkin pie spice). Cover and chill 8 hours. Serve with gingersnaps, apple or pear slices, or graham cracker sticks.

Victor Z Martin
2001

Tomatoes, Onions, and Peppers

Everyone wants tomatoes in the garden. They are the favorite crop of every home gardener, and even people who don't consider themselves gardeners stick a few tomato plants in the ground or in a pot in the spring. Tomatoes love sunshine and rich soil. Get them in as soon as danger of frost has passed, and keep them fed and watered. You want them to grow and produce quickly before the summer heat stops fruit set and stresses the plants to the point where the stinkbugs, leaf-footed bugs, and other pests descend. I spray my garden at least every two weeks with a blend of seaweed, fish emulsion, molasses, and other stuff—you can buy the blends or make your own (see "Recipes to Make Your Garden Bountiful"). Use a pump-up sprayer or hose-end sprayer to mix with water and spray away. This is a nutritious blend and won't burn tender new growth.

Peppers are another favorite crop, and you have a wide choice of heat levels available—anything from bell peppers to habanero peppers are happy to grow in the home garden. They like the same conditions as tomatoes but will often save the heaviest crop for late in the summer when the heat starts to mitigate a little bit.

Onions like cool weather in which to grow. They can go into a fall garden; you can plant seeds in the winter, or put in young plants in very early spring. Enjoy them green or dried—onions are the start of so many recipes, you can't do without them. You can also grow shallots, garlic, and chives, all onion relatives, in your garden and use them in your fresh recipes and in pickles as well. All of these goodies appear in the following favorite recipes.

RAINBOW SALAD

Select two or three small-fruited varieties of tomatoes with different colors. Some possibilities are Yellow Pear, Red Pear, Sugar Lump, and Maine Tomato Berry. Or choose slicers of different colors: Mr. Stripey, Mortgage Lifter, Cherokee Purple, and Old German.

If you are using cherry-sized tomatoes, cut in half and heap on a serving plate. If you are using slicers, arrange the slices on a plate, alternating colors. Finely chop half an onion and sprinkle over the tomatoes. Slice 3 large fresh basil leaves and sprinkle them over the onion. Salt and pepper lightly. Drizzle about one teaspoon olive oil over the tomatoes and onion, then dash on about ½ teaspoon wine vinegar. Let the salad sit at room temperature for a few minutes, covered, to let the flavors mingle before serving.

FRESH TOMATO PASTA

4 large or 6 medium-sized tomatoes (about 4 cups diced)
1 onion, chopped
2 garlic cloves, minced
1 tablespoon fresh or ½ teaspoon dried basil
2 tablespoons fresh or 1 teaspoon dried oregano
½ pound mozzarella cheese, cubed
2 tablespoons olive oil
1 tablespoon lemon juice
Salt and pepper to taste
1 pound of your favorite pasta
Parmesan cheese to garnish

Choose your most flavorful heirloom tomatoes and chop them into a large bowl. Add all other ingredients except Parmesan and pasta. Let sit, covered, at room temperature for an hour or so.

Cook and drain the pasta. Immediately add the hot pasta to the tomato mixture. Mix thoroughly and serve with a spoon so that none of the delicious sauce is lost. Pass Parmesan to sprinkle on top.

This is our favorite summertime dish and is infinitely variable. You can use toasted garlic bread instead of pasta to mix with the fresh tomato sauce and give it body. You can leave out the pasta and serve it with toasted bread on the side as bruschetta. You can use different kinds of cheese—Cheddar, feta, Munster, Gouda, pepper jack—to vary the taste. You can add cucumbers and peppers to the mix to add flavor and crunch. Just use your imagination and put in the ingredients you like best (or have in the fridge).

GAZPACHO

This is really a variation of the recipe above, but you eat it in a bowl and so it is soup!

4 medium tomatoes, chopped (and peeled if the skin is tough)
1 small onion, chopped
1 garlic clove, chopped
1 cucumber, seeded, peeled, and chopped
1 chopped pepper, hot or mild, depending on your taste
2½ cups tomato juice
Juice of one lemon
¼ cup olive oil
½ tablespoon salt
1 teaspoon pepper

Combine all the ingredients in a large bowl and cover. Mix and chill well before serving.

CEVICHE (A.K.A. CEBICHE OR SEVICHE)

Yet another chopped vegetable variation and really good!

   2 pounds fresh (*really* fresh, no fishy smell) firm-fleshed fish
       fillets—Red snapper is good, and you can also use shrimp or
       scallops, but always FRESH!
   1 small onion, chopped fine
   1 cup chopped tomatoes, peeled and seeded
   1 serrano or jalapeño pepper, seeded and chopped fine
   2 teaspoons salt
   1 tablespoon chopped fresh oregano
   ½ cup chopped fresh cilantro
   1 ripe avocado, sliced
   Tortilla chips

Place fish fillets, onion, tomatoes, and pepper in a glass or ceramic
dish—preferably a flat one so there is more surface available. Cover with
the lemon and lime juices, salt, and oregano, and then cover with plastic
wrap. Refrigerate for several hours so the flavors will blend and the fish
will "cook" in the acidic juices. Top with the cilantro and avocado as a
garnish. Serve with the tortilla chips. Restaurants often serve ceviche in a
sherbet or martini glass. It looks great that way, but it tastes terrific out of
a paper plate or anything else!

TOMATOES AND OKRA

   1 slice bacon, chopped
   ¼ cup minced onion
   2 cups sliced okra
   2 cups peeled and chopped tomatoes
   1 cup boiling water
   1½ teaspoons salt
   1½ teaspoons sugar
   Pepper to taste

Fry the bacon until crisp. Remove from the pan and set aside. Sauté onions in the remaining bacon fat until tender. Add the okra, tomatoes, boiling water, salt, sugar, and pepper, and cover the pan. Bring to a boil, then reduce the heat and simmer for 15 minutes. Stir occasionally to prevent sticking. When the okra is tender, serve with the reserved bacon sprinkled on top.

TOMATO-GARLIC QUICHE

1 pie crust (homemade or store-bought)
1 tablespoon olive oil or butter
1 small onion, minced
3 large cloves garlic, minced or put through a press
1 medium ripe tomato, peeled and chopped
1 additional tomato, sliced
1 tablespoon tomato paste
¼ teaspoon dry or 1 teaspoon fresh thyme
Salt and pepper to taste
3 large eggs at room temperature
1 cup milk
Dash of Worcestershire sauce
Pinch of nutmeg
1 cup grated Gruyère cheese
¼ cup grated Parmesan cheese

Prepare the pie crust and prebake 5 minutes at 350°F. Remove the crust and leave the oven on.

In a heavy skillet, heat the oil or butter and add the onion and garlic. Sauté over medium-low heat until tender. Add the chopped tomatoes and tomato paste and cook over low heat until reduced to a fairly thick sauce. Add the thyme and season to taste with salt and pepper.

Blend together the eggs, milk, Worcestershire sauce, and nutmeg. Stir in the cooked tomato mixture. Line the crust with the sliced tomato and pour in the custard mixture. Bake 30–40 minutes in the preheated oven or until a knife comes out clean. Let sit about 10 minutes before serving.

CORN-STUFFED PEPPERS

4–6 bell peppers, green or red (mature)
1½ cups corn kernels
1 cup diced raw tomatoes
4 teaspoons finely chopped celery
1 tablespoon finely chopped onion
2 tablespoons melted butter
2 eggs, lightly beaten
1¼ teaspoon salt
⅛ teaspoon pepper
½ cup soft bread crumbs

Wash the peppers, remove the tops, and scrape out the seeds and membranes. Parboil the peppers and tops in salted water for about 4 minutes. Drain the peppers. Combine the remaining ingredients and stuff into the peppers. (If the peppers won't stand up, cut a very thin slice off the bottom to make them level.) Put the tops on the stuffed peppers. Place the peppers into a greased casserole dish with a small amount of water in the bottom of the dish. Bake, covered, at 350°F for 50–60 minutes or until the peppers are tender and the stuffing is cooked.

JOHN WAYNE'S CHEESE CASSEROLE

I don't know if John Wayne ever made this, but the recipe was attributed to him when I got it 35 years ago and it's a keeper!

1 cup chopped mild green chilies (you can used canned if you don't
  have fresh)
1 pound Monterrey jack cheese, diced
½ pound Cheddar cheese, grated
4 eggs, separated
⅔ cup evaporated milk
1 tablespoon flour
½ teaspoon salt
⅛ teaspoon pepper
Tomato slices, enough to go around the edge of the dish

Preheat the oven to 325°F. In a large bowl, mix the chilies and cheeses. In a small bowl beat the egg whites until stiff. Beat the egg yolks lightly in yet another bowl and add the flour, milk, salt, and pepper. Blend well. Fold the yolks and whites together, then fold the eggs into the chilies and cheese mixture. Place in a buttered 9 × 13-inch casserole dish. Bake 30 minutes, remove from the oven, and arrange tomato slices around the edges of the dish, slightly overlapping. Bake 30 minutes more. More green chilies can be sprinkled on top. Let sit a few minutes after taking out of oven before serving.

Recipes to Tide You Over the Winter

For the Freezer and the Pantry

Keep the garden-fresh taste going even after the garden is gone! Some of these recipes will take a little more time, effort, and equipment than fresh-cooked dishes, but you will be able to enjoy and share your garden year-round.

TOMATOES FOR THE FREEZER

When your tomatoes are coming in fast and furious, you can save them for winter soups, stews, sauces, and other cooked dishes by simply freezing them.

Wash ripe tomatoes and cut them in half. If there are blemishes, cut them off. Place the tomato halves on a baking sheet and put it in the freezer. When the tomatoes are frozen solid, take them off the sheet and put them in a plastic freezer bag. Remove as much air as you can. The tomato halves will be waiting for you when you're ready to cook up a tomatoey treat in the dead of winter. You can do the same thing with peppers and strawberries.

TOMATO SAUCE FOR THE FREEZER

This is a recipe that can be expanded or shrunk depending on how many tomatoes you want to use up. It is great for that time when tomatoes are ripening almost faster than you can pick them, but you want to save the flavor for the winter. Just add proportionally more onions, garlic, and herbs if you have more tomatoes than this recipe calls for.

    2 tablespoons olive oil
    1 onion, chopped
    3 garlic cloves, chopped
    4–6 cups chopped tomatoes, with stems and blemishes removed
      but peels and seeds left in
    ¼ cup fresh basil, chopped
    ¼ cup fresh oregano, chopped
    Salt and pepper

Sauté the onion and garlic in the oil until translucent. Add tomatoes and cook over medium-low heat until the tomatoes become pretty mushy. Add basil, oregano, salt, and pepper and continue to cook for 10 minutes or so. Let cool. You can put the sauce through a blender or food processor now or when you thaw the sauce. The skins and seeds of the tomato are full of taste but aren't particularly great for the texture of the sauce, so it does need blending. Pour the sauce into a freezer container and seal. Usually containers that hold a quart, or 4 cups, are a convenient size for using later in the year. Pints work well for small families. When you need some great summer taste, just thaw, heat, and pour over pasta or add to your favorite recipe.

TOMATILLO SAUCE FOR THE FREEZER

1 pound tomatillos
1 cup chopped onion
4 garlic cloves
1½ teaspoon salt
½ cup oil
1 cup water
½ cup cilantro (or more to taste)
2 serrano peppers (or more to taste)

Cut the tomatillos in half and place in a blender or food processor
with the other ingredients, reserving 2 tablespoons of the oil. Heat the
reserved oil over medium heat in a heavy pan, then add the puréed
tomatillo mixture. Simmer on low heat for 10–12 minutes. Serve as a dip
with tortilla chips, use in a recipe, or pour into pint containers and freeze
for later use.

Herb Butters

Herbs blended into unsalted butter or margarine make one of the
easiest and most satisfying ways
to use and preserve herbs. Simply
soften the butter or margarine and
add the chopped or crushed herbs.
Herb butters can be shaped and
given as gifts and are easily stored
in the freezer wrapped in plastic
wrap until you are ready to use
them. You can add the butter to
sauces, soups, gravies, pasta, rice,
and vegetables, or dot on fish or
meat. Here are some good herb and
butter combinations: {dill, mustard,
parsley} {sage, parsley, chives} {tar-
ragon, fennel, parsley, lemon zest}
{salad burnet, garlic chives, parsley}
{savory, marjoram, parsley}.

Pestos

Having frozen pesto in the house is like having a readymade dinner anytime you want. Thaw and serve over pasta or vegetables or with crackers
and you'll immediately be transported back to the peak time of garden
tastiness.

Don't limit yourself to traditional basil pesto, either. You can use flavored basil—lemon, cinnamon, spicy—or you can use parsley, spinach,
or other green goodies to make different flavors of pesto. Experiment
with the basic recipe and discover your own garden favorite. Vary the
kind of nuts and cheese you use to change the flavors. You can have pesto
for dinner every night and not once repeat the taste!

SPINACH PESTO

2 cups firmly packed spinach leaves
2 cloves garlic
¼–½ cup olive oil
½ cup grated Parmesan cheese
⅓ cup toasted pecans

Combine the nuts and garlic in a food processor and whir until finely ground. Add the spinach and continue to process until coarsely chopped. Pour the oil into the mixture through the top and continue to process until the mixture is finely chopped but not puréed or mushy. Stir in the cheese. Add salt and pepper to taste.

Pesto freezes beautifully. Put it into serving-size containers or into ice cube trays for individual servings. Remove the cubes when frozen and put them into a plastic freezer bag.

SOUTHWESTERN PESTO

Substitute cilantro and pistachio nuts for spinach and pecans in the recipe above. If you can find a firm Mexican cheese, use it instead of Parmesan. Follow the directions above and serve with burritos, quesadillas, or enchiladas.

SAGE PESTO

½ cup fresh sage leaves
1½ cups fresh parsley
2 garlic cloves
½ cup toasted pine nuts
½ cup Parmesan cheese
½ cup olive oil

Combine the sage, parsley, garlic, cheese, and pine nuts in a food processor. Process to mix. With the machine running, add the oil until the consistency is right. Tuck a tablespoon of Sage Pesto under the skin before baking chicken breasts or use as an ingredient in holiday bread stuffings.

૪

At one time in our history, home canning was one of the few options available to people who wanted to have fruits and vegetables out of season. Women canned throughout the summer so that they and their families could eat throughout the winter. Today we have the luxury of buying fresh and preserved food year-round.

Still, it is sometimes rewarding, frugal, and enjoyable to can your own homegrown vegetables. The primary danger involved in canning is from botulism, which can and does result in serious illness and even death. To avoid any problems, you need to learn the rules of home canning. You may want to use a pressure canner or boiling water baths, and you need to know which foods need additional acid, which ones to pack hot, and which ones cold. Find a good book on home canning or check the Internet or your county extension service for detailed instructions on how to can safely. Don't ever eat canned food if the seal has come undone, if there is mold growing on the food when you open it, or if it has been sitting around more than one year. If you haven't canned foods before, or even if you have, you need to learn the safety rules. They are easy and accessible.

Low-acid foods like green beans for example must be processed in a pressure canner. A boiling water bath will work for jams, jellies, and high-acid recipes like salsa and pickles. Even if your grandma's jelly recipe doesn't mention boiling water baths, you should process all your canned foods after they are in the jar to make sure all bacteria is dead. Follow directions carefully when processing your food. You want to enjoy this stuff, not keel over from it!

If you want to make jelly or pickles but don't want to bother with the hot water bath ritual, simply make them and store them in the refrigerator. Eat them up quickly and there will be no problems.

CANNED TOMATO SALSA

7 quarts fresh tomatoes (paste-style hold up best), peeled, cored, and chopped
4 cups chopped mild peppers (green or red)
5 cups chopped onion
½ cup hot peppers, seeded and finely chopped
6 garlic cloves, finely chopped
2 cups lemon juice

2 tablespoons salt
1 tablespoon black pepper
2 tablespoons ground cumin
3 tablespoons chopped oregano leaves
2 tablespoons fresh cilantro

Combine all the ingredients except the oregano and cilantro in a large pot and bring to a boil, stirring frequently. Reduce the heat and simmer 10 minutes. Add the herbs and simmer for another 20 minutes or so until the salsa is the desired consistency. Stir frequently. Ladle the hot sauce into pint jars, leaving ½-inch headspace. Adjust the lids and process in a boiling water bath for 15 minutes. This will make about 13 pint jars.

Note: Do not increase the amount of peppers in the recipe. If you want it hotter or milder, change the varieties of peppers used. Mild varieties are bell, Anaheim, ancho, college, Colorado, Hungarian yellow, and long green chilies. Hot varieties are jalapeño, serrano, cayenne, habanero, and tabasco.

BLACKBERRY VINEGAR

3 cups fresh or frozen blackberries
1 gallon white distilled vinegar
3 tablespoons sugar

Place the berries (reserve about ½ cup) in a large, wide-mouthed jar or other nonreactive, closeable container. Return the reserved berries to the freezer. Warm the vinegar and pour over berries and sugar. Cover the jar loosely and allow it to stand for 8 days, shaking or stirring gently daily. If you'd like a sweeter brew, add some sugar to taste. Strain the vinegar. Using a funnel, pour the vinegar into decorative bottles. Add some of the reserved berries to each bottle and seal tightly. These make great gifts if you have more than you can use yourself.

HERB VINEGAR

Making herb vinegars is incredibly easy and the results are tasty, versatile, and will impress your friends. You can make vinegar out of a single favorite herb, such as basil. Opal basil makes beautiful pink vinegar that has the fresh flavor of basil and is good added to salads or soups or used to baste meat or vegetables while they are cooking. Or you can combine favorite flavors like basil, thyme, and oregano for a nice Mediterranean flavor. Experiment and mix and match. Herb vinegars make great gifts when they are put into decorative bottles. You can also experiment with vinegars—white, wine, rice, or your other favorites—to change the flavors.

Place clean (washed AND dried) fresh herbs into a clean quart jar with a lid. Fill the jar loosely with herbs. Pour the vinegar over the herbs and put on the lid. Place the jar in the pantry or on the windowsill or on the counter—someplace where you will remember to shake it every day or so. After a month, strain out the herbs and put the vinegar into a bottle. Herb vinegars don't have to be refrigerated, but I usually do keep mine in the fridge just in case.

Good herbs to use in vinegars include bay leaves, basil, rosemary, oregano, thyme, tarragon, garlic, and dill.

HERB SALT

Herb salt is a healthful addition to soups, stews, dressings, meats, and vegetables. The simplest means of making it is by combining equal amounts of salt and any combination of ground-up fresh or dried herbs. Paprika, red pepper, or dry mustard may be added for further flavor and color.

1½ teaspoon each of dried thyme, bay leaves, black pepper, and nutmeg
¾ teaspoon each of cayenne pepper and marjoram
3 teaspoon powdered cloves
3 teaspoon salt

Mix together all ingredients. Shake on food before or after cooking.

SOS (SAVE ON SALT) SEASONING

1 teaspoon chili powder
1 tablespoon garlic powder
2 teaspoon ground oregano
6 tablespoons onion powder
3 tablespoons paprika
2 tablespoons dry mustard
3 tablespoons poultry seasoning
2 teaspoons black pepper

Combine all the ingredients and mix well. Spoon into a shaker. Yields about 1 cup.

PICKLES

Most people think of cucumbers when they think of pickles, and indeed you can't beat a good cucumber pickle on a big, fat hamburger. But there are plenty of other great vegetables that make terrific pickles. It is just a matter of changing your perspective.

With more and more people growing their own and shopping for fresh vegetables at the farmers' market, there is new interest in ways to preserve seasonal produce. If you want to eat local and healthily, preserving some of the crop when it is plentiful and economical is the way to go. Using bottled water in pickling is a good idea since tap water often has many minerals that may discolor your veggies. Also, use pickling salt to maintain the proper proportions.

RED AND GREEN PICKLES

   3 pints tomatillos (or you can use green tomatoes)
   3 pints firm red tomatoes
   3 large onions
   3 red sweet peppers

3 bunches celery (or to taste)
½ cup kosher or pickling salt
1 teaspoon cinnamon
1 teaspoon ground cloves
½ cup mustard seed
3 pints vinegar
4 cups sugar

Chop the tomatillos, tomatoes, onions, peppers, and celery. Add the salt and let sit at least 6 hours or overnight. Drain and rinse with clear water. Put into a large pot and add the remaining ingredients. Cook until the vegetables are tender. Ladle into sterilized jars and top with sterilized lids. Process in a boiling water bath for 45 minutes. Makes about 12 pints.

CB

Squash—Like its relative the cucumber, squash makes great pickles. If you have ever grown zucchini, you know how that crop can get out of hand in a hurry. Instead of sneaking around in the dark of night to leave baskets of zucchini on your neighbor's porch, turn your bountiful harvest into tasty treats. You can substitute firm, young squash in almost any cucumber pickle recipe. If you grow long, skinny heirloom English or Armenian squash, you get the flavor of squash when you cook them and the look of cucumbers when you pickle. Be sure you choose firm squash for pickling. Mushy vegetables make mushy pickles and nobody likes mushy pickles! Another consideration is the size of the seed. Big seeds aren't tasty in pickles. This is another good reason to choose a long, slender squash with minimum seeds.

SUNSHINE SQUASH PICKLES

BRINE:
12 cups apple cider vinegar
12 cups water (use bottled water to avoid all the minerals in tap water)
1 cup pickling salt

Bring the brine to a boil, then let it cool.

Squash slices to fill about 4 quart-size jars
1 or 2 garlic cloves
1 hot pepper
1 bunch of dill

Fill sterile quart jars with the sliced squash. Add the garlic, hot pepper, and dill; then fill the jars with brine. Set the jars in full sun for 11–15 days until the jar lid pulls down and seals. (You can also process in a boiling water bath for 30 minutes.)

MIXED VEGETABLE PICKLES

BRINE:
¼ cups pickling salt
1 quart water

1 quart small cucumbers
2 cups pickling onions, washed and trimmed
2 cups cauliflower, cut in small pieces
2 cups carrots, peeled and cut in ¾-inch pieces
2 cups string beans, stem end and strings removed
⅓ cups white mustard seed
1½ cups sugar
1½ quarts vinegar

Cover the vegetables with the brine. Let stand overnight. Drain, cover the vegetables with clear water and let stand for 2 hours. Drain, cover with a mixture of the sugar and vinegar, and let stand overnight.

Drain off the vinegar mixture and heat it to simmering. Add the vegetables and simmer 15 minutes. Pack in hot jars; adjust lids. Process 10 minutes in a boiling water bath. Yields 4–6 pints.

∽

Garlic—Who hasn't heard about the benefits of garlic? Many people say it's good for your heart, good for your blood pressure, good to fight infections, and generally makes you feel better. On the other hand, most of us really don't want to chomp down on a clove of garlic for an afternoon snack. The solution is simple—garlic pickles! Garlic is easy to grow and produces a plentiful harvest. You can plant garlic cloves anywhere—in the vegetable garden, in the flower garden, around fruit trees, or along the fence. It will make a lovely plant early in the spring (or in the winter if you live in the South) and give you plenty of garlic to enjoy year-round. It is best to plant garlic in the fall and harvest it in the spring. Check with your local garden authority to make sure about planting time, but when you harvest, all you have to do is pull up the bulb, separate it into cloves, remove the paperlike skin, and proceed with the recipe if you are ready to use the garlic. Most of the garlic, however, will need to be allowed to dry slowly in a shady, dry spot. Pull up the bulbs, set or hang them in a spot where the breeze will dry any attached soil and let the outside of the bulbs become paperlike. Then store the bulbs in a dry place where the air can circulate around them. A basket works for storage as does simply hanging the bunches from the ceiling. You can remove the stems once the bulb has dried. The flowers will dry naturally and be lovely additions to a dried bouquet or alone. I keep a bunch on the porch for decoration and to leave the lingering scent outdoors! Here is a beautiful recipe for pickled garlic, but you can also use a regular dill pickle recipe and process the pickles in a boiling water bath to preserve them longer.

PICKLED GARLIC

6 ounces distilled white vinegar
6 ounces water
2 teaspoons pickling salt
⅛ teaspoon Old Bay Seasoning*
6 large garlic bulbs, separated, blanched, and skinned
Rind of 1 lemon, peeled in one continuous spiral
1 dill head or ½ teaspoon dill seeds
1 small red chili pepper, whole

Combine the vinegar, water, salt, and Old Bay Seasoning and bring to a boil in a nonreactive pan. (Stainless steel and enamel pans will not react to the salt and vinegar in the mix.) Add the garlic and let it steep 10 minutes over very low heat. Line a clean 1-pint jar with the lemon rind and add the dill and pepper. Ladle in the garlic and enough liquid to cover it. Cap and seal. Cool at room temperature, then store in the refrigerator for up to a month. Wait 3–4 days before using to allow the flavors to blend.

*If you can't find Old Bay Seasoning, make your own using a pinch each of celery seeds, cayenne pepper, ground cinnamon, ground ginger, allspice, ground yellow mustard, and paprika plus ½ bay leaf.

Cauliflower—one of the cool weather crops, cauliflower makes a tasty low-calorie pickle. If you have a big garden, you may find yourself overrun with cauliflower. It usually isn't a vegetable the kids want every night for dinner. Still, it is good for you and a beautiful vegetable. Turning it into pickles is easy and frugal.

PICKLED CAULIFLOWER

3 cauliflower heads, cut into small florets and washed (about 10 pounds)
8 cups distilled white vinegar
8 cups water
¼ cup pickling salt
2 tablespoons mustard seeds
12 garlic cloves
12 dill heads
12 small chili peppers

Steam the florets over boiling water for 1 minute. Simmer the vinegar, water, salt, and mustard seeds in a 5-quart nonreactive pan for 5 minutes. Pack six sterile 1-quart jars with 2 garlic cloves, 2 dill heads and 2 chili peppers. Pack warm cauliflower in each jar, leaving ¼-inch headspace. Cover with the vinegar solution, leaving ¼-inch headspace. Cap and seal. Process for 15 minutes in boiling water. Store the jars for at least 3 weeks before using to allow flavors to develop.

CB

Green beans, brussels sprouts, tomatoes, peppers, beets, and of course cucumbers all make wonderful pickles which can be used as a side dish, appetizer, party food, or fabulous gift. Great-Grandma may have had to preserve food to keep the family going, but we can do it just for the fun and the taste of it!

Preserves and Jellies

YELLOW PEAR TOMATO PRESERVES

 7½ cups Yellow Pear tomatoes
 6 cups light brown sugar
 1 large lemon
 1 navel orange
 ½ teaspoon salt
 1 teaspoon ground ginger
 1 stick cinnamon

Wash the tomatoes and remove their skins by dropping the tomatoes
into boiling water for 1 minute, then plunging them into cold water. The
skins should slip right off. Layer whole tomatoes with sugar in a large
bowl. Cover and leave in the refrigerator for six hours or overnight.

 Thinly pare the lemon and orange peel. Using only half of each peel,
cut it into slivers and set aside. Remove and discard the white pithy
underpeel and slice the lemon and orange. Remove the seeds. Cook the

slices with the reserved peel slivers in a scant amount of water for 10 minutes.

In a large cooking pot (enamel or stainless steel), combine the tomato-sugar mixture, the fruit mixture, and the salt, ginger, and cinnamon. Boil gently until the tomatoes are clear and the syrup is thick.

While the preserves are cooking, sterilize six 8-ounce jars. You can seal the jars with either fruit-jar lids.

When the preserves are ready, remove the cinnamon stick and skim off foam with a metal spoon. Fill the jars with preserves and seal. Process for 15 minutes in a hot water bath.

JUJUBE BUTTER

An informal survey several years ago showed that most people, if given the choice, preferred jujube butter to apple butter on their morning toast.

6 pints fresh ripe jujubes, halved
5 pints sugar
2 teaspoons ground cinnamon
Juice of 1 lemon
1 teaspoon ground nutmeg
½ teaspoon ground cloves
¼ pint white distilled vinegar

Place the halved jujubes in a saucepan with just enough water to cover. Boil gently until the fruit tender. Press the fruit through a sieve or colander to remove the skin and seeds.

Combine the fruit with the remaining ingredients and cook slowly until the mixture is thick.

Put the mixture in sterile canning jars (6 pint-size or 12 half-pint), leaving ½-inch headspace. Wipe the rims of the jars, cover with lids, and screw on the bands. Process in a boiling water bath for 15 minutes. Remove and cool at room temperature.

HERB JELLY

3 cups apple juice
1 cup fresh herb of your choice
2 tablespoons lemon juice
1 package powdered pectin
4 cups sugar
Fresh herb sprigs for decoration

In a covered saucepan, bring the apple juice and herb to the boiling point, but do not boil. Remove from the heat and let sit, covered, for 20 minutes. Strain the juice through a paper coffee filter or jelly bag, squeezing the herbs to extract all the flavor. Mix the flavored juice with the lemon juice and pectin. Bring to a full, rolling boil. Stir constantly. Add the sugar. Continuing stirring and return to a full rolling boil. Boil hard for 1 minute. Remove from the heat. Stir and skim off foam. Immediately pour into hot, sterilized jars with the herb sprigs in the bottom of each. Seal. Process in a boiling water bath for 15 minutes. Yields about 40 ounces.

You can experiment with different fruit juices or water and herb combinations. (Don't leave out the lemon juice. It is necessary.) You can also add food coloring to make your jelly a brighter color. Mint jelly is traditionally colored green. Opal basil will make a lovely rose color all by itself.

Recipes to Make You Feel Better

Remedies, Tonics, and Mosquito Repellents

This is not medical advice—just old-fashioned lore that keeps being validated by new-fashioned users. These recipes are based on traditions that have served people well for years, but if you are really sick, go see a doctor!

HERB TEAS FOR WHAT AILS YOU

To make herbal tea, bring 1 cup water to a boil. In a cup, place crushed dry herbs or chopped fresh herbs and pour boiling water over the herbs. Be sure the herbs are clean and potent. If they have been dried so long

as to lose their scent, they are too old. Use roughly twice as much fresh herb as you do dried. Let steep with the saucer on top of the cup to hold in warmth for about 10 minutes. Remove the saucer, strain out herbs, sweeten with honey if you wish, and sip the tea. Here are some herbs that through the years have been said to have beneficial effects:

Lemon balm tea is said to reduce anxiety and restlessness. A cup before bedtime helps you drop off to sleep. Use 1 tablespoon of leaves per cup of boiling water.

Passionflower tea is a traditional sleep aid. Said to help you drift into a restful sleep, the tea may be good for insomnia. Use 1 teaspoon dried or 1 tablespoon fresh herb per cup.

Peppermint tea has been known for generations as a digestive aid. Use 1 tablespoon of mint leaves or more per cup of water if you are feeling gaseous, nauseated, or generally suffering from an upset stomach.

Rosemary tea is said to be good for preventing headaches caused by stress. Use 1 teaspoon dried or 1 tablespoon fresh rosemary per cup of water.

Sage tea may sometimes be helpful in eliminating night sweats and is also used for coughs and colds. Use 4 tablespoons of dried sage in 1 cup water and steep for four hours or more. Strain, then drink.

Thyme tea is said to relieve cough, bronchitis, and sinus pressure. Sip the tea to help relax bronchial spasms that trigger coughing spells. Use 2 teaspoons of dried thyme per cup of boiling water and steep for 10 minutes.

UPSET TUMMY TEA

2 cups boiling water
1 teaspoon chamomile flowers
1 teaspoon lemon balm leaves
½ teaspoon catnip leaves
½ teaspoon fennel seeds

Pour water over the herbs and
steep for 10 minutes. Strain and
cool. Sip as needed for colic, nausea, and upset stomach. Good for
children.

UPSET TUMMY TEA 2

Basil tea is said to aid digestion. If
you drink it after a heavy meal, it
will help you feel less full. Just pour
boiling water over a few basil leaves
and let steep for about 5 minutes. Relax, and sip and you'll soon feel better. Basil leaves steeped in wine are also said to create a general tonic to
make you feel better all over.

UPSET TUMMY TEA 3

4 cups water
2-inch piece of fresh gingerroot
Honey and lemon to taste

Peel the gingerroot and slice into thin slices. Bring the water to a boil in
a saucepan. Once it is boiling, add the sliced ginger; reduce the heat and
simmer. Cover and cook over low heat for 15–20 minutes. Strain out the
ginger and serve. Add honey and/or lemon to taste.

Ginger has shown the ability to stop nausea and dizziness in several clinical trials and is being investigated as an anti-inflammatory agent in the treatment of arthritis. Ginger tea can be used for many kinds of stomach upset, from morning sickness to travel sickness. If you like spicy tastes, you can chew a small piece of a root to deter travel sickness. The tea is also said to be good for flatulence, poor circulation, and colds and flu.

SOOTHING BATH

If you have the sniffles, mix up this concoction of dried herbs for your bath:

    1 ounce borage
    2 ounces elder
    1 ounce burdock
    1 ounce mugwort
    ½ ounce bay leaf
    1 ounce eucalyptus
    1 ounce horehound

Mix the herbs thoroughly. Cover one cup of herbs with water and simmer for 10 minutes. Strain and add the tea to your bathwater. The bath should be warm, not hot. Wrap up in a cozy robe after bathing and slip into a warm bed. (If you don't have all the herbs, use the ones you do have.)

MOSQUITO SPRITZ

    2 cups catnip leaves
    3–4 cups mild rice vinegar

Rinse and dry the catnip; crush and place in a clean quart jar. Cover with the vinegar. Seal the jar and store in a dark place for two weeks. Shake the jar every day or so. Strain the liquid into a clean jar and refrigerate for up to 6 months. Use as needed by pouring a small amount into a spray bottle and spraying on exposed skin and around outdoor sitting areas.

CATNIP AND ROSEMARY MOSQUITO CHASING OIL

2 cups catnip leaves
1 cup rosemary, cut into 6-inch sprigs
2 cups grapeseed oil or any light body-care oil

Crush the herbs and pack into a clean jar. Cover with the oil, close the jar, and place in a cool dark place for two weeks, shaking every day or so. Strain the oil into a clean jar, cover and refrigerate up to 8 months. To use, rub the oil on exposed skin.

LEMON GRASS MOSQUITO REPELLANT

4–5 lemongrass stalk bases, chopped
1 cup vodka

Place lemongrass stalk bases and vodka in a blender and whir until well combined. Strain and add ½ cup water. Put into a spray bottle and mist yourself and your kids and pets to keep mosquitoes away. Store in the refrigerator.

BATH TO SOOTHE ITCHING

  1 cup peppermint leaves, minced
  ¼ cup lavender flowers or ½ cup
    minced lavender leaves
  4 cups colloidal oatmeal
  1 cups Epsom salts

Mix all the ingredients in a large bowl.
Add about 4 cups of hot water and
let soak for at least 30 minutes. Strain
the liquid and add it to a lukewarm
or cold water bath, or mix together
in water and sponge onto affected
area. Good for poison ivy, poison oak,
allergies, chicken pox, or whatever
itches you.

POTASSIUM BROTH

  2 large potatoes, unpeeled and
    chopped
  1 cup unpeeled sliced carrots
  1 cup unpeeled chopped beets
  1 onion, unpeeled and chopped
  1 cup chopped celery, including leaves
  1 bunch parsley

Placed the scrubbed, unpeeled, chopped vegetables in 1½ quarts of water.
Bring to a boil; reduce heat and cover. Cook slowly for 30 minutes. Let
stand for another 30 minutes. Strain the liquid off and drink it as broth.
This is packed full of minerals and is a great energizer. Add the cooked
vegetables to the compost heap.

HERBAL HEALING SALVE

If you are allergic to any of these ingredients, don't use them.

2 ounces dried comfrey leaves
1 ounce dried calendula flowers
2 cups olive oil
1 ounce pure beeswax
4 drops tea tree oil
4 drops lavender oil
1 ounce echinacea tea
1 ounce goldenseal tea

Heat the comfrey leaves and calendula flowers in the olive oil over low heat for about 5 hours. Do not let the mixture bubble. If you can't lower the heat enough to keep from bubbling, turn it off and on. Strain off the olive oil while it is still warm. Put 1¼ cups of the olive oil in a pan; add the beeswax and heat it just enough to melt. Add the essential oils and stir. Pour in jar and store at room temperature. Use for minor scrapes, burns, and other ouches.

If you aren't growing comfrey in your garden, give it a try. I have found it to be a wonderful herb for soothing scrapes and scratches. Just tear off a leaf and wrap the injured spot, and it will feel better in no time.

DRAWING OINTMENT

Jar of bland ointment or cream, such as calendula cream
Dried mullein leaves

Pulverize the leaves and stir into cream or ointment until it is thick and dark green. My kids call this "dirt cream" because it is sort of gritty and looks like dirt. I think it's great for any sore that seems to need an astringent or drawing effect—bites, pimples, splinters, or scratches and scrapes.

REJUVENATION SPICED TEA

3 cups water
2 two-inch pieces of cinnamon stick
1 teaspoon cardamom
20 whole cloves
3 cups milk
3 peppercorns
1 tablespoon chopped peppermint leaves

Combine the water, cinnamon, cardamom, and cloves. Bring to a boil and cook for 3 minutes. Reduce the heat and add the milk, peppercorns, and peppermint leaves. Heat almost until boiling. Remove from the heat, cover and let steep for 10 minutes. Strain; sweeten with honey to taste. This tea gives you energy and is said to open breathing passages, improve circulation, and generally rejuvenate the system. It tastes a lot like chai tea. Only the peppermint leaves will be found in the garden, but most of the other ingredients are in your spice rack.

Recipes to Make Your Home More Enjoyable

MOTH REPELLENT SACHET

1 cup rosemary
1 cup artemisia
1 cup pennyroyal
5 whole bruised bay leaves

Mix all ingredients together and tie into cheesecloth bags. Place among clothes in drawers or closets.

ALL-PURPOSE HOUSEHOLD CLEANER

½ cup distilled white vinegar
¼ cup baking soda or 2 teaspoons borax
½ gallon warm water
2 teaspoons soap or detergent
Sprigs of rosemary for scent and
  antibacterial properties

This solution can be used for a multitude of cleaning jobs, including countertops, floors, walls, rugs, and upholstery. Mix thoroughly and pour into spray bottle. Use a large sprig of rosemary so it won't clog the sprayer.

AN EVEN SIMPLER HOUSEHOLD CLEANER

Select an herbal vinegar with a smell you enjoy and mix in equal parts with water in a spray bottle. Use it to clean sinks, toilets, tubs, and many other surfaces. The acetic acid in vinegar kills viruses, germs, bacteria, and mold. It also dissolves mineral deposits and stains. Don't use it on marble.

USES FOR HERB VINEGARS

You can do many things with herb vinegars:

Place a bowl containing ½ cup of herb vinegar and 2 cups of water in your microwave and cook on high for 5 minutes to steam out the inside. Let cool in the appliance and then remove the bowl and wipe out the interior.

Wipe out your fridge with the vinegar and remove any accumulated mold from door gaskets. Follow with a sponge dipped in the same fragrance for freshness and hygiene.

Take down your shower and tap heads and soak them overnight to remove the mineral buildup for better, cleaner flow.

Freshen and disinfect all your dishcloths and sponges by soaking them overnight in water with at least 1 cup of herb vinegar and a couple drops of lemon essential oil. Rinse out and dry.

Freshen and disinfect your dishwasher with ¾ cup herb vinegar in the rinse cycle. This will also make your glasses sparkle.

INDOOR BUG KILLER

Mix 1 pound of diatomaceous earth with 4 ounces of orange oil. A pastry blender or wire whisk will help with blending. Use this to control roaches, ants, and any other indoor pest. Smells good and is less toxic to people than many insect killers are.

HERBAL AIR FRESHENER

1 cup dried peppermint
1 cup dried pineapple sage
½ cup orange peel
1 cinnamon stick

Place all ingredients in a pan containing 6 cups water. Simmer gently on the back burner, replacing water as it disappears.

BAY LEAVES FOR BUGS

If you grow a bay tree in your garden or in a container, you'll have plenty of leaves to use for many purposes. One great way to use bay is in the kitchen to repel unwanted bugs. The leaves put into canisters of grains (flour, cereal, rice, cornmeal) will repel weevils and miller's moths that love to sneak in and mess up your food. Simply placing leaves on the shelves and floor of the cabinet or pantry will also repel cockroaches. The bay leaves have a nice, subtle scent and will dry slowly, continuing to repel nuisance pests for a long time.

POTPOURRI

One of the nicest things about growing a garden is having at your fingertips the raw materials to use for so many things. Those same bay leaves that are repellent to bugs are very appealing to people. They make beautiful wreaths and add a wonderful scent to potpourri.

Potpourri has been used for centuries to make homes smell better. Today, making your own potpourri is easier than ever because you can stop by a craft or health food store and pick up small bottles of essential oils to suit your likes.

Before starting your potpourri project, decide on a theme. Do you want mostly roses? Seashells to remember your trip to the beach? Pinecones to complement Christmas decorations? Kitchen smells to make the house smell like comfort food? Or maybe citrus to give a taste of the tropics? Whatever you decide will determine which material you'll need to gather.

Here are the things you'll need:

4–5 cups fragrant dried plant material
⅓–½ cup dried citrus peel
4–5 tablespoons crushed spices
4–5 drops essential oil
2 tablespoons orris root
Textured elements
Large nonmetal mixing container and nonmetal spoon

Plant material can be any kind of plant from your garden that smells good—rose petals, lavender, lemon balm, sweet pea, rosemary, or anything you like. Remember, all the material must be thoroughly dried or you'll have compost instead of potpourri. So start your project by drying things, either in a dehydrator, in the microwave, or slowly in the fresh air. You can also add brightly colored flowers or flower petals to add color even if they don't have much scent. Tansy flowers, bachelor's button, gomphrena, rose hips, and tiny rosebuds are good choices.

The citrus peel can be orange, lemon, grapefruit, kumquat, or lime, and you can also include slices of dried citrus in the mix. They are pretty and colorful and add a nice, fresh scent. Dry the citrus by slicing thinly and either air drying or using a dehydrator or very slow oven. If you want to dry only the peel, be sure to remove all the white part of the fruit next to the peel.

Select your spices based on what you like: cinnamon, nutmeg, or cardamom are popular choices. Grind them to release the fragrant oils.

The same is true of essential oils. Based on the major scent you are going for in your potpourri, select your oils accordingly. If you want a floral scent, choose rose or lavender. If you like citrus, choose lemon or orange. Spend some time with those little jars sniffing and choosing.

Orris root is derived from iris plants and is available at most craft stores. It is used to hold the scent in your material. You don't want to go to all this effort and have it all smell good for a day and then be gone.

Texture is the larger pieces of material that will determine how the potpourri looks rather than how it smells. It can be pinecones or seashells or tree bark or sweet gum seedpods. Look around and see what is available in your garden and go from there.

Once you have your materials collected, start mixing them in your big nonmetal container. Sniff as you go and keep adjusting amounts of the different materials until you are satisfied. Pour the mixture into a covered container—a big plastic tub with a lid is perfect. Store it for 4–6 weeks in a cool, dark place to let all the smells come together in a nice blend. Shake the container every couple of days to get it nicely mixed.

Once it is "done," put your finished product into bowls, jars, or baskets and let them fill your home with good smells. Of course, homemade potpourri is also a wonderful gift in a fancy container or just a cellophane bag tied with a ribbon and a label showing that you are sharing your garden with your friend.

SIMMERING POTPOURRI

If you'd prefer to make a simmering potpourri that you can simply put on the stove and enjoy, here is one recipe. You can create your own by mixing and matching flowers, herbs, and spices:

1 cup scented pink rosebuds and petals
1 cup scented red rosebuds and petals
1½ cup orange peel, cut and sliced thin
16 whole nutmeg pods, whacked with a hammer
¼ cup whole allspice
1 tablespoon real vanilla
¼ cup fenugreek seeds
¼ cup whole cloves
¾ ounce rose essential oil

Mix all ingredients thoroughly. To use the potpourri, combine two tablespoons of your mix with two or more cups of water. Place in a potpourri simmering pot or simply put on your stove in a pan over very low heat.

Make sure the water doesn't all cook away. Store the unused portion in the refrigerator until you are ready to use it. This potpourri adds fragrance and bit of moisture to the air as well.

DECORATIONS

The most common, easiest, and perhaps most beautiful decoration you can add to your home is a bouquet of flowers and/or herbs straight from the garden. Whether it is artistically arranged in a Waterford vase or crammed into a repurposed peanut butter jar, a bouquet of freshness just can't be beat to cheer up a room and everybody in it. What mother hasn't lovingly arranged a collection of stemless weed flowers in a toothpick holder to acknowledge the gift of small, grubby hands? Bringing the garden indoors just comes naturally to people, young and old.

So cut some roses or daisies or irises or whatever else is blooming at the time and enjoy them in your home. In the winter, you can gather bouquets of evergreens to let you know that nature is still alive and kicking. I keep a stoneware pitcher full of bay leaves on the kitchen table all winter—the same stems—and it smells good, looks good, and is ready to be harvested for the soup without my even having to go outside.

If you want to go a little farther with your decorations, however, wreaths are a great idea. You can use wreaths in any room of the house or on the outside of the house if you prefer. You can make wreaths for every season and for every purpose. Culinary wreaths, herbal wreaths, spring wreaths, holiday wreaths—the choice is yours.

I love to give culinary wreaths to people who cook. These can be as simple as a wreath made entirely of bay leaves. They are beautiful, dry naturally, and smell good. They can be very small or very large, depending on your time, energy, and the size of your bay tree.

I make simple bay wreaths by attaching the leaves to the base with pins and overlaying them so that no pins are visible and the base is completely covered. That's it. No other decoration is needed. One year I made small ones for everyone to take home from a Christmastime luncheon, and they were a big hit.

Or you can get fancier and add other edibles from your garden: rosemary, lavender, sage, garlic, peppers, and more. Of course, this all assumes that you garden organically and are not putting nasty things on your plants in the garden.

If you don't even want to think about cooking, there are still lots of choices of wonderful plant material to include in your wreath. The process is the same for any plant material.

First you need to get a base for your wreath. Craft stores and big box stores usually have straw or twig wreath bases available in a variety of

sizes. You can, of course, make your own if you have lots of time and energy. Here is what you need for a mixed floral or herb wreath:

Wreath base
Reel of florist wire
Rubber bands (small)
Wreath pins, floral picks, or ordinary straight pins
Garden clippers
8- to 10-inch pieces of your favorite herbs and flowers, fresh and/or dried

The easiest way to make a wreath is the bundling method. Select either boxwood, rosemary, or another evergreen plant to use as your base, then start your bundles. For one bundle, for example, put the rosemary on the bottom and add other plants in a pleasing arrangement. The stem size of the bunch should be about as big around as a quarter. Secure your bundle with a rubber band (maybe two) to hold the plants in place. Clip the stems so they are even and start a pile of bundles. Keep making bundles, adding different accents to each one. You'll need about 20 bundles for a 10-inch wreath.

Once your bundles are made, put a loop of wire on the back of your wreath base to use to hang up the wreath. Then, starting at the top of the wreath, lay your bundles on and secure them by wrapping the floral wire around the stems and the base. Put on the first bundle and secure it, then add the next, overlapping so that the bottom of the stems don't show. Keep going around the circle. Secure the bundles well with several wraps of wire and keep the bundles facing in the same direction. If you don't like the way it looks, change it up as you go.

After all the bundles are in place, check to see if any rubber bands are showing or too much stem is visible. Cover these with sprigs of rosemary or whatever base you are using by just poking it in here and there. To add accents at this point, such as flowers or gumdrops, peppers or garlic, simply bend the stems and hold them in place with floral picks or pins.

Some people use hot glue in the construction of wreaths, but if you do that you will no longer have a wreath that can be used for cooking or eating. If you want to add a raffia bow, now is the time. Use your imagination and have fun. This is a project you do for fun, not as a required course!

If you don't want your wreath to be edible, go ahead and use that hot glue gun. For holiday wreaths, you can attach dried fruit slices, pomegranates, cinnamon sticks, gingerbread cookies, tiny artificial birds or birdhouses, Santa, elves, or whatever else strikes your fancy.

Living wreaths are another option. These are built on floral foam in a pot plant saucer, plate, or other flat container. Simply get a wire wreath frame in the size you want and stuff it full of pieces of foam (Oasis), soak it well so that it is full or water, place it on your flat container, and start arranging. Marge Clark, of Oak Hill Farm, used this method for many years to decorate the base of an antique crackle glass globe that sat on her coffee table. She used sprigs of fresh rosemary to cover the foam and added a bow on one side. You can also make one to fit around your punch bowl or a candleholder. You can use any flowers or herbs from your garden that you enjoy. I've seen beautiful ones made of small succulent plants in different shapes and sizes. Keep it watered and it will stay fresh for a nice long time.

Recipes to Enhance Your Body

The foundation of every lotion is an oil-and-water–based combination. You can vary the kind of oil you use depending on your skin type. Some good organic oils can be found at a health food store: sweet almond oil, grapeseed oil, apricot kernel oil, jojoba, sesame, and sunflower oils.

Begin the process of making your herbal oil by infusing your oil with the herb of your choice. Select one of these herbs to make a softening and smoothing lotion: aloe vera, jasmine, calendula, rose petals, or comfrey. If you'd like a lotion to use for massage or aches and pains, choose from these herbs: lavender, calendula, ginger, chamomile, St. John's wort, and rosemary.

Chop the herbs finely and place them in a glass jar with a tight-fitting lid. Pour enough oil into the jar to cover the herbs and seal. Place the jar in a cool, dark place and leave it alone for at least 1 week—longer to make the herbal infusion stronger. Pour the oil and herbs through a fine strainer, pressing the herbs to extract their potency.

BASIC LOTION

¼ cup herbal oil
⅓ cup distilled water
2 tablespoons shaved or grated beeswax

Place the herbal oil and beeswax in the top of a double boiler and heat until the beeswax is melted completely. Place the mixture in a blender and blend, adding the distilled water a little at a time, until it reaches the lotion consistency you prefer. (To make herbal creams, add more beeswax and less water.) Add essential oil, drop by drop, for added fragrance if you wish, adding enough essential oil to attain the strength of fragrance desired.

Homemade herbal body lotion will keep its freshness for a month to six weeks, perhaps longer, depending on the oil chosen. For example, jojoba oil has a longer shelf life than apricot kernel oil. Because herbal lotion is so easy and inexpensive to make, it's fun to create different recipes and fragrances to fit your mood and varying skin conditions and needs.

GINGER COLOGNE

1 generous handful of sweet-smelling ginger flowers
1 quart jar
Cheap vodka

Put a handful of ginger flowers into a quart jar and fill with vodka. Screw on the lid and store out of the sun. Shake every day for two weeks or so. Sniff and see if the scent pleases you. If it is not strong enough, add more flowers and repeat the process. When the scent is right for you, strain out all the flowers through cheesecloth or a paper coffee filter and store the cologne in the refrigerator. Splash on the cologne to enjoy the heavenly fragrance.

HERBAL BATH BAGS

Place a mixture of oatmeal, marjoram, lemon balm, chamomile, and pennyroyal into an inexpensive washcloth. Tie with a long ribbon and hang on the faucet in the tub. Let warm water run through the bag and use it to rub on aching muscles.

HERBAL HAIR CONDITIONER

⅓ cup each: rosemary leaves, chamomile flowers, raspberry leaves

Pour 1 quart of boiling water over the herbs and allow to steep for 20 minutes. Strain the mixture, cool, and pour the liquid over freshly shampooed hair, catching the liquid in a basin. Repeat five to ten times, making sure that all your hair has been covered. Dry your hair as you would normally.

Recipes to Make Your Garden Bountiful

BASIC INSECTICIDAL SOAP

1–2 tablespoons liquid soap (not detergent) such as Ivory or
  Dr. Bronner's
1 quart water

Mix well and spray as needed to kill and repel insect pests. To this mix
you can add strong-smelling roots, herbs, and spices. Make a tea of ginger, garlic, cayenne, horseradish, and other herbs with strong scents and
mix with the soap. Spray to repel insects, deer, and rabbits.

GARLIC SPRAY

Repels pests in the garden.

Mix 5 cloves of garlic with 2 cups of water in the blender. Blend well.
Add 1 tablespoon of liquid soap and stir until dissolved. Strain into a
sprayer that dilutes the mixture at a ratio of about 1 part garlic juice to
20 parts water or more. You can add hot pepper to this recipe plus a little
mineral oil if you wish to add more punch. If you add fish emulsion and
seaweed, you'll get even more benefits. (Fish emulsion is said to keep
rabbits away as well as adding fertility.)

HOT PEPPER SPRAY

Repels pests in the garden.

Blend 3–5 hot peppers in water. Strain and mix with a gallon of water.
Keep it off your hands and out of your eyes. Spray on plants to deter
insects. It also helps deter larger critters such as raccoons, dogs, and cats.
It might work on armadillos, but probably not.

HERBAL INSECT SPRAY FOR PLANTS

Brew ½ cup each of fresh thyme, sage, epazote, and garlic (use ¼ cup dried herbs) in a quart of water for 30 minutes. Strain and allow to cool. Spray on affected plants.

FUNGICIDE FOR PLANTS

Mix 4 teaspoons (1 rounded tablespoon) of baking soda or potassium bicarbonate into 1 gallon of water. Spray lightly on foliage of plants suffering from black spot, powdery mildew, brown patch, or other fungal diseases. You can also add 1 cup milk to enhance the solution and add calcium.

FIRE ANT (AND MORE) FORMULA

This is the original Garden-Ville formula for fire ants given to me by Malcolm Beck. It is now sold as Auntie Fuego Soil Conditioner. It works on a number of other insects and as a general tonic for the soil.

    1 part orange oil
    1 part (agricultural-grade dry or wet) molasses
    1 part liquid humic acid

Combine all ingredients and shake thoroughly to emulsify the orange oil. You can use compost tea instead of humic acid, but it makes the orange oil more difficult to blend. Mix with water before applying on ant mounds.

JOHN DROMGOOLE'S FERTILIZER MIX

3 tablespoons liquid fish fertilizer
1 tablespoon liquid seaweed
1 tablespoon molasses
1 tablespoon Medina soil activator

Mix all ingredients in 1 gallon of water and pour over plants, saturating the leaves and soil well. (You can also buy this fertilizer readymade wherever Lady Bug products are sold.)

ALFALFA MEAL TEA FOR ROSES

Mix 2 or 3 cups alfalfa meal in 5 gallons of water. Let steep in the sun for 2–3 days, stirring occasionally. Strain. Use approximately 1 gallon of liquid for each mature rosebush. Pour around base of plant. Work in any dregs left in the bottom of the bucket around the base of the plants.

TRANSPLANT SOLUTION

1 teaspoon vitamin B-1
1 tablespoon seaweed concentrate
1 tablespoon fish emulsion
1 tablespoon molasses

Mix all ingredients in a gallon of water and soak your transplants thoroughly as soon as they are in the ground.

ROCK DUST MILK

Slowly add water to 1 cup of rock dust. Stir slowly until dissolved. Add to 1 gallon water, allow to sit, then strain into sprayer. This makes the food instantly available to the plants that are sprayed. Rock dust has very large amounts of calcium, iron, and magnesium as well as many minerals that provide a quick energy boost to plants. It also increases the beneficial bacteria count in the soil. Rock dust added to filtered water and turned into a milky liquid and sprayed onto foliage and soil is good. I suggest adding a dash of natural soap along with a dash of seaweed. A dash would be 1 tablespoon of powdered seaweed or 1 ounce of liquid seaweed per gallon of filtered water.

You can use rock phosphate, greensand, or other finely ground minerals.

HOWARD GARRETT'S JUICE

Per gallon of water:
1 tablespoon seaweed
1 tablespoon natural apple cider vinegar
1 tablespoon blackstrap molasses
1–2 cups manure compost tea
For more serious disease infestations, add:
¼ cup garlic tea
1 tablespoon Neem per label directions
1 rounded tablespoon baking soda or potassium bicarbonate

Add fish emulsion and/or a commercial biostimulant such as Medina, Agrispon, AgriGro, or Bioform for greater response. For iron deficiency, add 1 tablespoon chelated iron. Spray during the cool part of the day.

(You can also purchase Garrett's Juice at local nurseries or at www.dirtdoctor.com.)

BRAZOS HOUSE CHARD COCKTAIL

A little Happy Hour for plants that need a lift.

Strain leftover water (that has been allowed to cool) from boiled Swiss chard; pour directly around the base of a plant. Or, coarsely chop a bunch of Swiss chard leaves and place in blender. Add water to fill; whirl, strain, and apply as above.

Recipe from Dominique Inge, gardener and garden writer.

COMPOST OR MANURE TEA

There is some debate about how to make compost tea. Some say just soaking compost in water is the natural way:— Nature drops stuff on the ground;, it rots;, rain falls, and the resulting rich broth feeds the plants.

Others say you have to add air to the compost brew in the form of some sort of mechanical bubbler. I'm going to tell you both ways, and you can decide which is right for you.

ɞ

The basic soak-it-in-water method: Place several shovels full of compost or manure into an old pillowcase, burlap bag, feed sack, or other fabric bag. Submerge in water—a large garbage can is good for this—for several days. (If you want to make smaller amounts, use a pantyhose leg as your "teabag" and a 5-gallon bucket of water.) It will steep more quickly in the sun. It will not smell wonderful, so locate it at some distance from the back door. Dip out the tea and use it to foliar feed all kinds of plants. You can use the "teabag" over again until the liquid is very light in color. Dump the remaining solids around the base of the plants. This is an all-purpose soil builder and also builds resistance to disease and insects.

ɞ

The more sophisticated aerated method: You'll need an aquarium pump large enough to run three bubblers or air stones, several feet of tubing, a gang valve, three bubblers, a stick for stirring, unsulfured molasses, a straining cloth (e.g., pillowcase, burlap bag, or feed sack), and a 5-gallon bucket. You can get the supplies at any store that sells aquarium supplies.

If you are using city water, fill another bucket of water and run bubblers in it for about an hour to get rid of the chlorine. Once you have safe water, fill the empty bucket half full of compost. Don't pack it in; the bubblers need loose compost to aerate properly. Cut a length of tubing and attach one end to the pump and the other to the gang valve. Cut three more lengths of tubing long enough to reach comfortably from the rim to the bottom of the bucket. Connect each one to a port on the gang valve and push a bubbler into the other end.

Hang the gang valve on the lip of the bucket and bury the bubblers at the bottom, under the compost. Fill the bucket to within 3 inches of the rim with water, and start the pump.

For adequate aeration, be sure the bubblers sit on the bottom of the bucket, which is half filled with compost.

When it's going, add 1 ounce of molasses, then stir vigorously with the stick. The molasses feeds the bacteria and gets the beneficial species growing really well. After stirring, you'll need to rearrange the bubblers so they're on the bottom and well spaced. Try to stir the tea at least a few times a day. A vigorous mixing with the stick shakes more organisms loose and into the tea. Every time you stir, be sure to reposition the bubblers.

After three days, turn off the pump and remove the equipment. If you leave the tea aerating longer than three days, you must add more molasses or the good organisms will start going to sleep because they don't have enough food to stay active. Let the brew sit until the compost is pretty much settled out, 10 to 20 minutes, then strain it into the other bucket or directly into your sprayer. You'll have about 2½ gallons of tea. If you want, this is the time to add foliar micronutrients, like kelp or rock dust. Use the tea right away, within the hour if possible. Add the solids to the compost heap to start the process all over again.

CONTAINER PLANT FOOD

   10 pounds compost
   1 pound rock dust
   1 pound alfalfa meal
   1 pound kelp meal or seaweed powder

Mix and feed container plants as needed, using 1 cup in a 5-gallon container.

NATURAL HERBICIDE

Spray undiluted 20% vinegar on the leaves of unwanted plants. Application may be repeated as necessary. Be careful to keep the vinegar off plants you want to keep.

CORNELL SPRAY FORMULA

Treats blackspot and powdery mildew.

   2½ teaspoons Ultrafine Sunspray Oil
   1 tablespoon Palmolive liquid
   1 tablespoon fish emulsion or liquid seaweed*
   4 teaspoon baking soda
   2–3 drops SuperThrive

Mix all ingredients with 1 gallon water. Spray weekly only as needed.
   *Be sure there is no added sulfur as it reacts chemically with the horticultural oil.

ALGAE REMOVER

Sprinkle whole-ground cornmeal in birdbaths, in fish bowls, on brown patch, and anywhere algae or fungus grows. The meal stimulates microbes that consume the algae.

BUG JUICE

I have to admit I haven't tried this. It is just a little too icky for me, but lots of people swear by it, so here it is:

Catch several grasshoppers or crickets and put them in your blender. Blend ½ cup of bugs in 2 cups of water. Strain and spray on plants to repel infestation. The theory is that bugs will smell the other bugs and assume the plants are already occupied. This can be frozen if you have a large bunch of bugs to process at one time.

A PILE OF MANY COLORS: MAKING YOUR OWN COMPOST

Mother Nature is the original composter. In the autumn of the year, old leaves, flowers, and twigs fall to the ground and begin to rot. Throughout the year, insects and microbes work on the debris and reduce it to useable nutrients for next year's plants. In the forest or the plains, if people don't intervene, nature takes its time creating new soil from the old stuff. This part of the process is essential. It is nature's way of creating fertile soil and healthy plants.

Without the fallen seeds, there would be no new plants next year, and

without the fallen leaves and other debris, the soil would have no way to replenish itself. That's the way it works in nature, but of course, we don't ever let nature just work. We have to intervene—clean up the fallen leaves, sweep away the pollen and seedpods, pick up and throw away faded flowers. Our tidiness often results in depleted soils and sick plants.

What we need to be doing instead of sending plant material to the dump is putting it into compost heaps. You can make compost in a variety of ways, some simpler than the others, but all easy. Composting is just one more step in the natural cycle. Plants naturally sprout from seed, bloom, die back, and compost. Then they sprout again and the cycle continues.

CB

You can make your compost heap as simple or as elaborate as you wish. A pile of leaves in the corner of the yard is a compost heap if you leave it alone long enough for the leaves to rot and turn into soil again. Or you can build a system of bins from wood and wire and move your compost from one bin to another as it progresses. Most people settle for something in between these two extremes.

It is helpful to have some sort of container for your compost heap to keep it from blowing away and sprawling around on the yard. The container can be a big tomato cage, a ring of hardware cloth or chicken wire, wooden pallets set on edge, or a garbage can with holes punched in the bottom.

Compost is made up of two kinds of material—brown stuff and green stuff. (These are the technical terms; you can also call them carbon and nitrogen materials.) Brown stuff, which includes dried leaves, dead stems, sticks, straw, dried grass, and any other dead plant material, is the carbon source for your compost. Green stuff provides the nitrogen and is green plant material such as fresh grass clippings, kitchen vegetable waste, green plants you pull from the garden, weeds, and manures. There are all sorts of formulae for combining these two kinds of material, and if you become a compost devotee you can work out your favorite recipe. If you don't want to become that involved with your compost, you can just put what you have in the pile and not worry about proportions.

The biggest problem that can occur if you don't have enough carbon is that the pile can smell and attract flies. A pile with lots of green stuff and very little brown stuff is too fresh, and that's where the problems arise. In that case, just find some old leaves or straw and add them to your pile. Shredded paper will work, too. On the other hand, you have to have plenty of nitrogen to heat up the carbon components. Heat in the pile makes the materials break down more quickly.

You also must have some active bacteria in your compost pile to begin digesting the material. These bacteria occur in nature, but if you have been applying chemical pesticides, herbicides, or sometimes even chemical fertilizers, you may have killed off these beneficial critters. You can buy compost starter to make sure you have the bacteria you need to get the compost going. If you use fresh manure in your pile, it will provide the bacteria. Most authorities say to use only the manure from plant-eating animals—cows, sheep, horses, rabbits, chickens, etc.—and not from domestic animals like dogs, cats, and people. (Given the sort of things we're hearing that cows eat, however, I wonder.)

If you get manure from a local farmer, be sure to ask if the animals are given antibiotics or other drugs on a regular basis. If they are, keep looking for another source.

Once your pile is built, you can keep adding to it as materials become available. You can stir the pile occasionally and water it when it is really dry. Or you can leave it alone and let it rot at its own speed. I usually just leave it alone and dig out the finished compost from the bottom.

The resulting material is dark, earthy, good-smelling, and wonderfully rich. You can screen the compost through a coarse wire mesh to remove any large pieces of unrotted material and to make it look better. Or you can just toss the big pieces back into the pile and not worry about it. Again, it is up to you how much work you want to put into your compost. You can dig it into your garden or pile it on top as mulch—either way, it will make your soil healthier and your plants glad to be alive!

WORM COMPOSTING

A variation on the theme of home composting is worm composting. It is especially good for people who live in apartments, who don't have any lawn, or who live in a very cold climate. Worm composting bins live inside with you. They are interesting science projects for the kids, don't smell or make a mess, and give you great plant food.

You can buy containers just made for worm composting (vermiculture) or you can make your own. What you need is some sort of box—plastic, rubber, galvanized, or wood—with a lid. You have to ventilate the container by drilling holes in the top and the sides so the worms won't suffocate. The larger the container, the more worms you have room for. Pick a size that fits your space.

☙

Fill your box with thin strips of unbleached corrugated cardboard or shredded newspaper, straw, dry grass, or other similar material. This provides a source of fiber and keeps the box well ventilated.

Red wiggler worms are the best choice for your compost box. Buy them on the Internet or from a local source. Keep them in the box and don't throw them in the yard when you're done with them. They can upset the balance of nature in your garden.

Set your box off the ground using bricks, cinder blocks, cups, or whatever works for you. Sprinkle the surface of your mixture with water every other day. Feed your worms vegetable scraps at least once a week. Feeding lightly and often will produce more worms to get you off to a good start. Chopping up the food helps them digest it more quickly. Add more fibrous material about once a month as it disappears. You will start with a full bin of paper and soon it will be half full. Add more material then.

To harvest the compost, put on rubber gloves and start sorting. Shining a bright light on a clean sheet of newspaper or plastic will help as a sorting surface. Put handfuls of compost on the surface. give the worms a minute to run to the bottom of the compost, and then make two piles: compost and worms. Put your worms back in the bin with new food and fiber, and put your compost on your garden.

No matter which method you use, the result is wonderfully rich compost. Compost contains all the nutrients that were in the raw materials you added to the pile, and it is packed with microorganisms that keep your soil active and productive. Without those microbes, your plants are not able to get the minerals and other goodies they need to grow strong and healthy. Compost encourages native earthworms, which encourage root growth and also loosen and feed the soil. There is no fertilizer you can buy that will build your soil better or more quickly than compost. Compost feeds the soil as well as the plants—and, if you make it yourself, it is free! What more could you ask?

Index